Connecting With the Heart of God

Lynette Hagin

Unless otherwise indicated all Scripture quotations are taken from the *King James Version* of the Bible. Public domain.

Scripture quotations marked Amplified are taken from the *Amplified® Bible*. Copyright © 1954, 1958, 1962, 1964, 1965, 1987 by The Lockman Foundation. Used by permission. (www.Lockman.org)

Scripture quotations marked NIV are taken from *The Holy Bible: New International Version®. NIV®*. Copyright © 1973, 1978, 1984 by International Bible Society. Used by permission of Zondervan. All rights reserved.

Scripture quotations marked NKJV are taken from the *New King James Version*. Copyright © 1982 by Thomas Nelson, Inc. Used by permission. All rights reserved.

Scripture quotations marked NLT are taken from the *Holy Bible, New Living Translation*, copyright © 1996, 2004, 2007. Used by permission of Tyndale House Publishers, Inc., Wheaton, IL 60189 USA. All rights reserved.

Scripture quotations marked TLB are taken from *The Living Bible: Paraphrased* by Kenneth Taylor. Copyright © 1971 by Tyndale House Publishers. Used by permission.

Scripture quotations marked Message are taken from *The Message*. Copyright © by Eugene H. Peterson 1993, 1994, 1995, 1996, 2000, 2001, 2002. Used by permission of NavPress Publishing Group.

26 25 24 23 22 21 20 08 07 06 05 04 03 02

Talk to Me: Connecting With the Heart of God
ISBN-13: 978-0-89276-809-7
ISBN-10: 0-89276-809-6

Copyright © 2011 Rhema Bible Church
AKA Kenneth Hagin Ministries, Inc.
All rights reserved.
Printed in USA

In the U.S. write:
Kenneth Hagin Ministries
P.O. Box 50126
Tulsa, OK 74150-0126
1-888-28-FAITH
www.rhema.org

In Canada write:
Kenneth Hagin Ministries of Canada
P.O. Box 335, Station D
Etobicoke (Toronto), Ontario
Canada M9A 4X3
1-866-70-RHEMA
www.rhemacanada.org

All rights reserved. Contents and/or cover may not be reproduced in whole or in part in any form without the express written consent of the Publisher. The Faith Shield is a trademark of Rhema Bible Church, AKA Kenneth Hagin Ministries, Inc. registered with the U.S. Patent and Trademark Office and, therefore, may not be duplicated.

Contents

Introduction

My heart's cry and one of the things that I endeavor to do as I travel all over the United States and around the world is to create a desire within people's hearts to connect with the heart of God through prayer. There has been much teaching on prayer, and I praise God for that teaching. It's wonderful and it's been of great benefit to us because we need to know the principles of prayer. But we can hear sermon after sermon and teaching after teaching on prayer, and yet until we actually take time to pray—to talk to God—it's all to no avail.

Why is prayer so important? Because our destiny is determined by our prayer life. And prayer is what will take us where we need to go in life. You see, God is calling us to a higher level—a higher plane—in our communication with Him. In order to reach that higher assignment, we must connect with the Father as never before. Simply stated, He wants us to talk to Him.

That doesn't mean we have to spend three hours a day in prayer. Sometimes just a five-minute connection with the Lord and with the anointing of the Holy Spirit is what we need to see a dramatic difference in our lives. Even a few moments of pouring out our hearts to Him can sometimes propel us into His perfect plan!

Honestly, I believe that we, as Christians, are behind in our prayers. In so many cases, we have put prayer on the back burner. Really, I believe we've had the emergency brake on in the area of our prayers. We need to take the emergency brake off and give ourselves to prayer!

In these last days, we desperately need to catch up on our prayer life. If we want to see mighty demonstrations of God's power, we're going to have to communicate with Him. Then and only then will we step into our assignments. We will step into another realm of communion with our Heavenly Father. And we will take our place in the plan of God!

I pray that by the time you finish reading this book, I will have imparted to you a greater desire than ever before to talk to your Heavenly Father. And I trust that you'll be so inspired to pray that you won't be able to do anything else until you've spent some time communicating with Him!

That is my heart's cry. It's something the Lord has mandated me to do. It's so strong within me that sometimes I think I'm going to burst. The overwhelming desire of my heart is to stir up the people of God to get on their knees and pray!

CHAPTER 1

Knowing God in the Lions' Den

"The people that do know their God shall be strong, and do exploits."
—Daniel 11:32

These words from the Book of Daniel have been exploding in me for several years now. And every time I read them, the thought keeps growing stronger and stronger in me—it's so important for us to know our God.

The same passage in the *Amplified Bible* says, "*The people who know their God shall prove themselves strong and shall stand firm and do exploits [for God].*"

Daniel is referring in this scripture to the last days—the days right before the end of time—when the Bible says there will be much sin and darkness on this earth. And I believe the indications are all around us that we are living in the last days. Bible prophecy is actually being fulfilled right before our very eyes.

Daniel was saying that in these perilous times, even though many corrupt and wicked things may occur, those of us who know our God can stand firm on His promises. Conditions in our world may be growing worse. It may seem that darkness is about to take over this earth. But when we have a close relationship with our Heavenly Father, we can be strong in the Lord and do mighty exploits for Him!

Certainly in this day and hour it's more important than ever before that we stand firm. Even when the boat of our lives seems to be rocking and reeling, we must stand firm in the things of God.

You see, the enemy knows his time is short. That's why he is trying so desperately to tear down the Kingdom of God. He's trying to cause God's people to waver. He's trying to entice us into diluting the Gospel. But if we will be strong in the Lord and draw on the foundation we have in God's Word, this can be our greatest hour!

Daniel Was a Man of Prayer

When I think about knowing God, I always think of the prophet Daniel. Daniel was a man who knew his God. He was also a mighty man of prayer. Of course, in order to know the Lord, we must spend time talking to God—communing with Him in prayer.

Although Daniel was a captive in the land of Babylon, he still knelt down by his window three times a day and faced toward Jerusalem as he prayed to the Lord his God. In other words, he was faithful and consistent in his prayer life. It didn't matter what else was going on—Daniel always took time to pray.

It seems that Daniel's constant praying eventually began to annoy people. Did you know that when we pray, it stirs things up in the spirit world? And it also stirs up the devil!

Of course, the enemy is happy when believers are lukewarm. But he really gets upset when we begin to pray because he knows that prayer is the most powerful force there is against his kingdom. And Satan trembles at the weakest Christians on their knees in prayer!

Thank goodness Daniel realized the power of his prayers. Let's read more of his story from Daniel chapter 6.

DANIEL 6:1–4

1 It pleased Darius to set over the kingdom an hundred and twenty princes, which should be over the whole kingdom;
2 And over these three presidents; of whom Daniel was first: that the princes might give accounts unto them, and the king should have no damage.
3 Then this Daniel was preferred above the presidents and princes, because an excellent spirit was in him; and the king thought to set him over the whole realm.
4 Then the presidents and princes sought to find occasion against Daniel concerning the kingdom; but they could find none occasion nor fault; forasmuch as he was faithful, neither was there any error or fault found in him.

Why were these presidents and princes plotting against Daniel? Because they were jealous of him. Isn't it amazing what jealousy will do? You see, Daniel was full of the power of God and he also had a spirit of excellence. Sometimes people are jealous of those who excel.

DANIEL 6:5–7

5 Then said these men, We shall not find any occasion against this Daniel, except we find it against him concerning the law of his God.

6 Then these presidents and princes assembled together to the king, and said thus unto him, King Darius, live for ever.

7 All the presidents of the kingdom, the governors, and the princes, the counsellors, and the captains, have consulted together to establish a royal statute, and to make a firm decree, that whosoever shall ask a petition of any God or man for thirty days, save of thee, O king, he shall be cast into the den of lions.

Notice that these men told the king that *all* the presidents, governors, princes, counselors, and captains had consulted together to establish a royal statute. Let me ask you this: wasn't Daniel one of the three presidents? Of course he was. Was he included in that meeting? No, he wasn't. Guess what? They lied to the king, didn't they?

That tells me that we should always be careful when people are pressuring us to do something. We should also be extremely careful any time we sign a document, because we may not understand the full ramifications of what we are signing.

It's so important for us to pray that the hidden things will be revealed to us. Daniel 2:22 says, "*He* [God] *reveals deep and hidden things; he knows what lies in darkness*" (NIV). And Jesus said in Luke 8:17, "*For there is nothing hidden that will not be disclosed, and nothing concealed that will not be known or brought out into the open*" (NIV).

When we are making any type of decision, we need to ask the Lord to bring those secret things out into the open and reveal the hidden agendas to us. We also need to pray that whatever is in darkness will come to light.

Daniel Refused to Compromise

King Darius signed the decree which said that no one could pray to anyone besides the king for 30 days. When Daniel heard about it, did he change his routine? Absolutely not. He had no intention of compromising his relationship with the Lord, despite the king's decree.

What did Daniel do? He went to his upper room and prayed, as was his custom.

DANIEL 6:10

10 Now when Daniel knew that the writing was signed, he went into his house; and his windows being open in his chamber toward Jerusalem, he kneeled upon his knees three times a day, and prayed, and gave thanks before his God, as he did aforetime.

When Daniel heard about the king's decree, he could have said, "I'm just going to pray quietly for the next 30 days. I'm not going to open my windows as I've always done." Most of us probably would have thought, *Oh my goodness, not only am I not going to open my windows when I pray, but I believe I'll go into my prayer closet and shut the door!*

But Daniel was not ashamed of his relationship with the Lord. He didn't change his routine one bit, in spite of the king's decree. As far as he was concerned, it was just business as usual.

Why didn't Daniel change his routine? Because he knew his God! And he knew the Lord in such a way that he was absolutely certain his God would take care of him, regardless of what happened.

So Daniel continued praying to the Lord, and obviously he must have prayed loudly because the presidents and princes heard him. Those tattletales couldn't wait to report back to the king. They cried out, "O king, Daniel is disobeying your decree! He's praying every day to his God."

Of course, the king was terribly upset when he heard the news, because Daniel was his favorite among all the rulers of his kingdom. He deeply regretted that he had let the other rulers convince him to sign that decree. He hadn't understood the ramifications of what he was signing. But he paid royally for his decision.

DANIEL 6:14 (NKJV)

14 And the king, when he heard these words, was greatly displeased with himself, and set his heart on Daniel to deliver him; and he labored till the going down of the sun to deliver him.

The king tried desperately to find a way to change his decree. But according to the law of the Medes and the Persians, a decree that was signed by the king could not be reversed. Thus the king was forced to give the order for Daniel to be taken into custody.

DANIEL 6:16 (NKJV)

16 So the king gave the command, and they brought Daniel and cast him into the den of lions. But the king spoke, saying to Daniel, "Your God, whom you serve continually, He will deliver you."

Notice that the king had complete confidence in Daniel's God, even though he didn't serve the Lord personally. He had observed Daniel's devotion to his God, and it had made an impact on him. He had also seen the excellence of Daniel's spirit, and he knew it was because of his relationship with the Lord.

The king said, "Daniel, your God Whom you serve *continually* will save you." Can it be said of us that we serve our God continually? Can it be said that we commune with the Lord day and night? It's so important for us to know the Lord the way Daniel knew Him.

Notice that Daniel didn't wait until he was thrown into the lions' den to pray and talk to His God. He didn't wait until he was in the middle of a crisis to call upon the Lord in prayer. No! Daniel served God *continually.*

Some people only serve the Lord when disaster strikes. The only time they become fervent in their prayers is when they're in the middle of a huge crisis. They cry out to God and say, "If You'll just take care of this for me, I'll always serve You." But as soon as the crisis is over, they promptly forget all about the promise they made to the Lord. I'll tell you, we need to be careful not to forget the things that we have promised God!

A Night in the Lions' Den

After Daniel was cast into that den of hungry lions, a stone was brought to block the opening.

DANIEL 6:17–18 (NKJV)

17 Then a stone was brought and laid on the mouth of the den, and the king sealed it with his own signet ring and with the signets of his lords, that the purpose concerning Daniel might not be changed.

18 Now the king went to his palace and spent the night fasting; and no musicians were brought before him. Also his sleep went from him.

All night long the king tossed and turned. He couldn't sleep. He didn't even call for his musicians. But Daniel didn't have any trouble sleeping. He didn't sit there in the lions' den trembling and fearing. He didn't wonder, *Is my God going to deliver me? Am I going to be devoured by these hungry lions?*

Why was Daniel's heart not troubled? Why did he have so much peace? Because he knew his God. He had an intimate relationship with Him.

Now I'm going to let my imagination go for just a moment as I try to picture the scene that might have taken place in the lions' den that night. I can just imagine Daniel sitting there peacefully, resting in confidence because he knows those lions cannot hurt him. Why couldn't they hurt him? Because he was trusting in His God!

I can see him starting to get a little bored as he takes out his songbook and turns to the Book of Psalms. And then I can picture him as he begins to sing the 91st Psalm.

PSALM 91:1–2

1 He that dwelleth in the secret place of the most High shall abide under the shadow of the Almighty.

2 I will say of the Lord, He is my refuge and my fortress: my God; in him will I trust.

"*In Him will I trust.*" Daniel obviously took those words literally, didn't he? He was putting all of his faith and trust in his Savior.

Can you say in the midst of your lions' den, in the middle of your worst nightmare, "I dwell in the secret place of the Most High; I will say of the Lord, He is my refuge and my fortress. I'm going to put my trust in Him"?

There's so much comfort for us in the Word of God! There's so much comfort in knowing that when trouble strikes, our Heavenly Father takes us under His protecting wings.

As Daniel begins to sing the 91st Psalm, I can just picture him declaring, "Oh yes, I *do* dwell in the secret place of the Most High, and I abide in the shadow of the Almighty. He is my refuge and my fortress, and under His wings I shall trust."

I can imagine Daniel boldly confessing, "I will not be afraid for the terror by night or the arrow by day. I don't have to be afraid of any type of danger. My God will deliver me."

Then I can picture his faith welling up in him as he exclaims, "A thousand may fall at my side and ten thousand at my right hand, but it shall not come near me!"

By this time, I can just see Daniel absolutely shouting and rejoicing as he declares, "*No* evil shall befall me! My God will give His angels charge over me, to keep me in all of my ways."

Just as Daniel finishes singing those verses, I can picture one of those lions crouching down, getting ready to pounce. But Daniel proclaims, "I will tread upon the lion and the adder. I will trample the young lion and the dragon under my feet. My God will be with me in trouble. He will deliver me. With *long* life He will satisfy me and show me His salvation."

By the time Daniel finishes singing that psalm, those lions are so tame that I can just picture him saying to one of them, "Come on over here, Leo. I need to rest my head. Come be my pillow." And then I can see him looking over at the lady lion and saying, "Lucy, I'm cold. Come over here and keep me warm."

Daniel wasn't the least bit disturbed in his spirit by the predicament he found himself in that night. Even though he was surrounded by ferocious lions, he had no fear. He knew that his God would deliver him from every lion, even if there were a hundred lions gathered around him. He remained confident and at peace in the lions' den because he had a close, intimate relationship with his God.

When you have a close, intimate relationship with your Heavenly Father, you can be in the midst of any lions' den—any type of trouble or predicament—without fear. There may not be any literal lions surrounding you, but it may seem as if there are lions all around you.

You can stand on the promises of God, speak His Word, and know that those promises are not going to fail you. And you can refuse to camp in the valley of trouble and distress because you know that your God is going to deliver you out of all the distresses and troubles of your life.

That's exactly what happened to Daniel that night. God sent His angel to close the lions' mouths and Daniel remained safe in the lions' den all night long. But the king was so concerned about him that he arose early the next morning and rushed to the lions' den to make sure Daniel was still alive.

DANIEL 6:20 (NKJV)

20 And when he [the king] came to the den, he cried out with a lamenting voice to Daniel. . . . "Daniel, servant of the living God, has your God, whom you serve continually, been able to deliver you from the lions?"

Notice the words again—"*whom you serve continually.*" Those are very important words. The king was saying the same thing he had said in verse 16—that Daniel was a man who continually served the Lord.

DANIEL 6:21–22 (NKJV)

21 Then Daniel said to the king, "O king, live forever!

22 My God sent His angel and shut the lions' mouths, so that they have not hurt me, because I was found innocent before Him; and also, O king, I have done no wrong before you."

Daniel was kept from all danger in the lions' den that night because he knew his God. He was protected because he knew that God was his refuge and his defense in a time of trouble.

What happened to Daniel's accusers? The king not only threw *them* into the lions' den, but he also threw their wives and children in with them! Before they hit the bottom of the pit, their bones were crushed and the lions devoured them all!

Some have said that Daniel escaped from the lions' den because those lions didn't have any teeth. But if they didn't have any teeth, how on earth did they devour Daniel's accusers?

Of course those lions were ferocious! Certainly they had the ability to kill. They tore Daniel's accusers to pieces before they hit the bottom of the pit.

Why didn't the lions kill Daniel? Why was he preserved from danger? Because he knew his God. Because he prayed and talked to the Lord continually and served God faithfully all the days of his life. Daniel's close relationship with his God is what kept him safe from all harm!

Do You Know Him?

I want to ask you today: How well do you know your God? Can you say, as the old hymn says, that He "walks with me, and He talks with me, and He tells me I am His own"?[1] I'll tell you what, in the sweetness of the day, in the sweetness of the night, as you walk with the Lord and talk with Him, He will give you the strength you need for any task in your life—any trial, any lions' den, and any situation that comes your way!

Do you know your God the way Daniel knew Him? Do you know Him so well that you can rest in confidence, no matter what befalls you, knowing that the Lord will deliver you out of every snare of the enemy?

There's a ferocious lion prowling this earth—the enemy of your soul—and he is seeking to destroy you (1 Peter 5:8). But if you will boldly rise up and declare, "My God will deliver me! My God will do exceedingly abundantly above all that I can ask or think," the Lord will rescue you. And like Daniel, you will rise to the top!

Of course, knowing God doesn't mean that you will never go through tests, trials, or tribulations. As long as you're here on this earth, there are going to be tests, there are going to be trials, and there are going to be tribulations. But if you will put your trust in your Heavenly Father and walk close to Him, He will deliver you out of them *all*!

CHAPTER 2

A Heavenly Father or a Heavenly Lifeguard?

The Lord desires so much for us to know Him, for our hearts to connect with His, and for us to long for fellowship with Him. But in many cases it seems that the only time we're inspired to pray is when something awful happens to us. During those times it's easy for us to pray fervently.

The instant trouble strikes, we cry out, "God, please help me! I'm sinking. I need a lifeguard!" And God, in His grace and mercy, lifts us up. But for some of us, the *only* time we call upon the Lord is when we need a Heavenly Lifeguard. When everything is going smoothly, we're simply not inspired to talk to Him.

It must grieve the Father's heart when we fervently and earnestly communicate with Him only when we push the 911 button—the panic button. It must hurt Him as well when we're motivated to pray only when we have a need—"Father, I need this," or "Lord, I need that." We commune with God only as our Heavenly Butler.

I wonder if the Lord gets tired of hearing those kinds of prayers. He might prefer to let those calls go directly to His voice mail.

Have you ever thought about what God's voice mail might be like? Perhaps He would say something like this:

"Thank you for calling My Father's House. Please select from one of the following options. Press one for requests. Press two for thanksgiving. Press three for complaints. Press four for all other inquiries.

"I'm sorry—all of our agents are busy assisting other sinners right now. However, please stay on the line. Your prayer is important to us, and it will be answered in the order it was received.

"If you would like to speak to God the Father, press one. For Jesus, press two. For the Holy Spirit, press three. If you would like to hear King David sing a psalm while you're holding, press four.

"To find out if a loved one has been assigned to Heaven, press five, then enter his or her social security number and press the pound key. If you get a negative response, try area code 666.

"For reservations at My Father's House, please enter J-O-H-N followed by 3-1-6.

"For answering nagging questions about dinosaurs, the age of the earth, and where Noah's Ark is, please wait until you arrive here.

"Our computers show that you've already prayed once today. Please hang up and try again tomorrow.

"This office is closed for the weekend to observe a religious holiday. Please pray again after 9:30 a.m. on Monday. If you need emergency assistance when this office is closed, contact your local pastor."[2]

Thank goodness, God loves us so much that He never puts us on hold and He never lets voice mail pick up our calls. But He *does* desire for us to talk to Him—to come to Him even when we don't have any requests and tell Him, "Father, we love You so much. We're so thankful for all of Your blessings." He wants us to commune with Him and spend time with Him. Above all, He longs for us to get to know Him better!

Knowing God Through His Word

Our Heavenly Father knows us so well because He's the One Who created us. But how do we get to know Him? One of the most important ways we can get to know the Lord is by meditating in His Word. Oh, the Word of God is so precious! If we want to know our God, we need to fall in love with His Word.

At RHEMA Bible Church where my husband and I are pastors, we give the babies in the nursery their own little Bibles. The teachers hold the Bible up to their cheeks and say to the children, "We love our Bibles." Why? We want those little ones to get acquainted at an early age with loving their Heavenly Father and His Word.

I remember hearing about one little boy from the church who was roaming around his house eagerly searching for something. But his mother didn't have any idea what he was looking for. Finally, his eyes lit up when he saw the big family Bible in the living room.

That precious little boy went over to that great big Bible and struggled to try to lift it to his cheek. Why? Because he loved his Bible so much. It's so important that we fall in love with our Heavenly Father through His Word!

God's Instruction Book

Joshua 1:8 in the *Amplified Bible* says, "*This Book of the Law shall not depart out of your mouth, but you shall meditate on it day and night, that you may observe and do according to all that is written in it. For then you shall make your way prosperous, and then you shall deal wisely and have good success.*"

"This Book of the Law" is the Bible, God's Word. I like to call the Bible God's instruction book. It tells us about His love, His compassion, and His mercy. It also gives us His promises, as well as our rights, benefits, and authority in Christ. It teaches us how to resist the devil and how to recognize the works of the enemy. It gives us the instructions we need to successfully live this life.

But how many of us really like to read instructions? I am especially aware that some men don't like to read instructions. How do I know that? I've lived with my husband, Ken, for over 45 years.

I remember one particular time when Ken was putting together a swing set for our children. He very methodically laid out all the pieces, but when he came to the instructions, he simply set them aside.

It was only supposed to take 30 minutes to put that set together, but after many hours of laboring, Ken still didn't have a swing set. He finally succeeded in putting together some semblance of a swing set. But when he was finished, he had a whole pile of pieces left over and he had absolutely no idea where they were supposed to go! Are you getting my point here?

Why does it take us twice as long as it should to get where we want to go in life? Because we're not following the instructions. It's vitally important for us to continually check God's instruction book!

Of course, on the other hand, if we ladies try to read the instructions on a piece of equipment or another product, sometimes we can't even remotely understand them. They're Greek to us!

One time my husband gave me a digital camera for my birthday. At first I didn't even try to use it because I hadn't read the instructions. When I finally had a chance to look at the instructions, I simply couldn't figure them out. So I handed my camera to one of the members of our crusade team and said to him, "Here are the instructions. See if you can understand them."

Much to my amazement, he just grabbed my camera, threw the instructions aside, and immediately started pushing buttons. I thought, *Men* are *all alike, aren't they!* Finally, as he continued to push the buttons while I read the instructions to him, we figured out how to use my camera and I was able to take a few pictures.

What is my point here? So often we do not take the time to read God's instruction book. Or, we may read the instructions, but we don't always understand them.

For example, the *King James Version* may be difficult for you to understand. If that's the case, I encourage you to try reading from a version that's easier for you. You can also pray Paul's prayer in the Book of Ephesians—that your eyes will be enlightened to the Word of God.

EPHESIANS 1:18–19

18 The eyes of your understanding being enlightened; that ye may know what is the hope of his calling, and what the riches of the glory of his inheritance in the saints,

19 and what is the exceeding greatness of his power to us-ward who believe. . . .

I have read certain scriptures over and over again in every translation I could find, and yet I still struggled to understand them. After I prayed that prayer from the Book of Ephesians, all of a sudden a light bulb seemed to flash on when I read those same verses. Why? Because the eyes of my understanding were being enlightened to the Word of God. Suddenly I was able to grasp what God was saying to me, and I could walk in the truth of His Word.

Have you ever read a scripture over and over again, and when you had a need, you turned to that same scripture and suddenly you saw something you had never seen before? The Lord ministered something special to you from the verses you had been meditating on.

Sometimes God will highlight just one word from a scripture. I always encourage people, when they meditate on God's Word, to emphasize one word at a time.

For example, if you're meditating on Philippians 4:19—*"But my God shall supply all your need according to his riches in glory by Christ Jesus"*—highlight the word *all.* As you meditate on that verse, remind yourself that it's not just *some* of your needs, *a few* of your needs, or your *biggest* needs that God has promised to fulfill. It's *all* of your needs!

The more you meditate on God's Word, the better you'll understand what He is saying to you. And as you meditate on

Him and receive His instructions, you'll find yourself walking more closely with Him!

The Bible Is Your Key to Life

It's so important for you to cherish your instruction book—the Bible—just as that little boy cherished the old family Bible and tried to hug it to his cheek. The Bible is your manual for living. It's your key to life!

I certainly treasure my Bible. You see, my Bible answers prayer better for me than any other Bible. Why is that? Because my Bible has been with me through so many rough times and tribulations, and I have so many verses in it highlighted.

When I look through the pages of my Bible, I can say, "This is where God spoke to me. Those are the words the Lord dropped into my heart." And I can hold on to those words and let them encourage my faith. His words of encouragement really stir my heart!

God's Word is so precious to me because even when there seems to be no specific answer to my prayers, His Word leads me and guides me. And He always speaks to me through His Word.

The more we read and study God's Word, the more we learn about the Lord. You see, His character and nature are revealed through His Word. When we read about the things Jesus did—healing the sick and setting the captives free—we can see what our Heavenly Father is like. Jesus said in John 14:9, "*He that hath seen me hath seen the Father.*"

In these last days, it's absolutely necessary for us to know our God through His Word. The more we know Him, the more we begin to realize that He is faithful and we can always depend on Him. Why is that so important? Because if we have a strong foundation of knowing God through His Word, we can stand firm, no matter what!

Knowing God Through Prayer

The Bible is God's instruction book, written to us, His children. But if all we do is read our instruction book and we never have any fellowship with the Lord, our relationship is not going to rise to the level where He desires for it to be!

Let me ask you a question. What if, in raising our children, we were to write an instruction book or a manual to help them grow up and prosper? If we gave them that manual and they followed it, they might turn out okay. But what would we miss? We would miss our fellowship with them! Our lives would be incomplete. Our relationship with our children would not rise to the level of closeness that we desire to have with them.

Really, we wouldn't have much of a relationship with our children at all if they never talked to us. Don't we, as natural parents, desire for our children to talk to us, just as we talk to them? God feels the same way about us, His children. And prayer is how we fellowship with and talk to our Heavenly Father. He is seeking for us to fellowship with Him!

JOHN 4:23 (NKJV)

23 "But the hour is coming, and now is, when the true worshipers will worship the Father in spirit and truth; for the Father is seeking such to worship Him."

It is through prayer that we talk to our Heavenly Father and He talks to us. It is through prayer that we can be ministered to by Him. And the more we seek Him, the more the windows of Heaven will be open to us—far more than we can possibly fathom!

When people say, "God never talks to me," it might be because they never talk to Him. In the natural, if we don't set aside time to communicate with our spouse, our children, or even our best friend, they're probably not going to talk to us either. Those lines of communication are going to shut down, and instead of growing closer, we will grow further apart.

Have you ever noticed how God's voice becomes faint when you're not spending much time communing with Him? When you feel as if the Lord seems so far away, just stir up your lines of communication and you'll feel that closeness you desire once again!

A Wireless Connection With the King of Kings

What do we usually do, in the natural, if we want to talk to someone? We call them on the telephone, don't we? Most of us today have cell phones, and those allow us to be in contact with almost anyone in the world at any time.

But do you realize that for hundreds of years, we have had a wireless connection with the most important Being there is—the King of Kings and Lord of Lords? How have we had that connection? Through prayer! But we haven't always taken advantage of our connection with the Father, have we?

We may wonder at times why we're living defeated lives. But one reason might be that we've failed to understand how important our connection is with the Lord. We've failed to understand the importance of knowing Him through our prayers.

Most of us hate to be without our cell phones. The same thing should be true concerning our prayer life. Once we realize how important it is for us to talk to the Father, we should feel absolutely paralyzed if we don't have a strong connection with Him through prayer!

How Well Do You Know Him?

How well do you know your Heavenly Father? There are some who only know the Lord as their Creator. For others, the only relationship they have with God is to know His Name. And even then they may only use that Name as a swear word.

Others have accepted Christ as their Savior, but their communication with the Father has stopped there. Their relationship hasn't gone any further than, "Thank You, Lord, I'm on my way to Heaven." But God wants more of a relationship with us than that!

Some know the Lord as their Deliverer, and that's wonderful. But God doesn't want our relationship with Him to stop there either. He also desires for us to know Him as our Healer. First Peter 2:24 says that Jesus Christ bore the stripes on His back so we don't have to be sick anymore.

And God wants us to know Him as our Provider—the One Who meets our needs. Philippians 4:19 tells us, "*My God shall supply all your need according to his riches in glory by Christ Jesus.*"

Most of all—more than anything else in the world—our Heavenly Father desires for us to know Him as our Best Friend. He's a friend who sticks closer than a brother (Prov. 18:24), closer than any other friend we could ever have. And He's a friend Who will never betray us. We can bare our hearts to Him, and He will keep what we tell Him a secret. He will always be there for us—to help us, support us, and undergird us at all times.

Oh, if we could only understand that our close, intimate relationship with the Lord Jesus Christ is the only thing that will truly relieve the stresses of this life. It's what will open doors of opportunity, lead us in the paths where we desire to go, and cause us to walk in His footsteps and His ways!

What should our heart's cry be? That we would know the Lord in a closer and more intimate way. That we would talk to Him and spend time in His presence. Above everything else in the world, our greatest passion in life should be to know our Heavenly Father!

CHAPTER 3

The Surpassing Greatness of Knowing God

The Apostle Paul is one of my greatest heroes in the Bible. When I think of all the things he endured to promote the Gospel—the beatings, a terrible shipwreck at sea, being stoned and left for dead on the side of the road, and being thrown into jail—I am amazed that everything he wrote was so positive and uplifting.

How could Paul say those encouraging things and really mean them in the middle of such adverse situations? How could he constantly uplift and encourage others when he was being cast down himself? He could do it because of his close, intimate relationship with his God. You see, Paul's greatest desire in life—his highest passion—was knowing Jesus Christ!

Let's read in the Book of Philippians what Paul had to say about knowing the Lord.

PHILIPPIANS 3:8 (NIV)

8 What is more, I consider everything a loss compared to the surpassing greatness of knowing Christ Jesus my Lord, for whose sake I have lost all things. I consider them rubbish, that I may gain Christ.

PHILIPPIANS 3:8 (Amplified)

8 Yes, furthermore, I count everything as loss compared to the possession of the priceless privilege (the overwhelming preciousness, the surpassing worth, and supreme advantage) of knowing Christ Jesus my Lord and of progressively becoming more deeply and intimately acquainted with Him [of perceiving and recognizing and understanding Him more fully and clearly]. For His sake I have lost everything and consider it all to be mere rubbish (refuse, dregs), in order that I may win (gain) Christ (the Anointed One).

Paul had an incredible relationship with his Heavenly Father, and yet he longed to know the Lord even more. And that should be our heart's cry each day—to know Jesus Christ even more than we know Him right now and to become progressively more intimately acquainted with our Savior.

In verse 10 of Philippians chapter 3, Paul repeats the same passion.

PHILIPPIANS 3:10 (Amplified)

10 [For my determined purpose is] that I may know Him [that I may progressively become more deeply and intimately acquainted with Him, perceiving and recognizing and understanding the wonders of His Person more strongly and more clearly], and that I may in that same way come to know the power outflowing from His resurrection [which it exerts over believers], and that I may so share His sufferings as to be continually transformed [in spirit into His likeness even] to His death.

Paul's greatest passion in life was to know Jesus Christ. And he didn't want to know the Lord on a merely superficial level. Why did he want to know God in such an intimate way? Because he knew that knowing the Lord was the secret that would cause him to triumph in every situation in life!

Paul knew that if he knew God more, not only would the Lord be with him, but God would be *everything* He had promised in His Word that He would be—his Provider, his Healer, his Strengthener, and his Deliverer. I'll tell you, when you know the Lord Jesus Christ in that way, it is such a blessing and a comfort to your heart!

When you know your Heavenly Father as Paul did, you can say in the middle of any trial or tribulation, "I always triumph in Christ Jesus" (2 Cor. 2:14). When you know the Lord as Paul knew Him, you can say, *"For I know whom I have believed, and am persuaded that he is able to keep that which I have committed unto him against that day"* (2 Tim. 1:12).

Paul's number-one priority in life was knowing Jesus Christ. That was what kept him in the midst of everything that happened to him. And that should be our total desire in life—to know our Heavenly Father more intimately, more completely, and more deeply than ever before.

The more we commune with the Lord, the more we will recognize His great love for us. We will know and understand that if He is concerned about a sparrow falling to the ground, He is so much more concerned about us, His children. Then, as we pour our hearts out to Him in prayer, we will know that we can trust Him and believe His Word. And we can rest assured that He is going to lead us down a wonderful road in life!

Instead of Asking, Paul Was Declaring

Notice in all of these verses we've read from the Book of Philippians that Paul wasn't asking the Lord for a blessing. In fact, if you think about all of his writings, he almost never asked for anything for himself.

Instead of asking, Paul was always declaring. He was always praising his God. He was always making his confession of faith concerning his Savior. It's amazing to me that no matter what happened to Paul, he faithfully declared what he knew about the Lord. Let's read the words he wrote in Ephesians chapter 1 to praise his Heavenly Father.

EPHESIANS 1:3–6 (NIV)

3 Praise be to the God and Father of our Lord Jesus Christ, who has blessed us in the heavenly realms with every spiritual blessing in Christ.

4 For he chose us in him before the creation of the world to be holy and blameless in his sight. In love

5 he predestined us to be adopted as his sons through Jesus Christ, in accordance with his pleasure and will—

6 to the praise of his glorious grace, which he has freely given us in the One he loves.

What is Paul doing in these verses? He's declaring what he knows about his Lord and Savior. And why does he know these things? Because he knows his God. He knows that his Heavenly Father is able to do exceedingly abundantly above all that he could ever ask or think. And the reason he knows it is that he continually communicates with the Father.

After Paul makes his declaration concerning what he knows, he asks God to give this revelation to the Ephesians.

EPHESIANS 1:15-20 (NIV)

15 For this reason, ever since I heard about your faith in the Lord Jesus and your love for all the saints,

16 I have not stopped giving thanks for you, remembering you in my prayers.

17 I keep asking that the God of our Lord Jesus Christ, the glorious Father, may give you the Spirit of wisdom and revelation, SO THAT YOU MAY KNOW HIM BETTER.

18 I pray also that the eyes of your heart may be enlightened in order that you may know the hope to which he has called you, the riches of his glorious inheritance in the saints,

19 and his incomparably great power for us who believe. That power is like the working of his mighty strength,

20 which he exerted in Christ when he raised him from the dead and seated him at his right hand in the heavenly realms.

Paul prays that the Ephesians might know the Lord better. Sometimes we think we already know God extremely well, but we should always have a desire to know Him even more. We should desire for His presence to be fresh and alive in our hearts 24 hours a day!

When we know our Heavenly Father in a close and intimate way, if we encounter difficult situations, we can start declaring the victory right in the middle of the problem. Why? Because we already know what the outcome will be. We already know the end result—the Word says that we are more than conquerors through our Lord and Savior, Jesus Christ (Rom. 8:37).

We can declare to the enemy, "Greater is He that is in me than he that is in the world" (1 John 4:4). And we can boldly say, "I can do all things through Christ Who strengthens me!" (Phil. 4:13).

Why can we declare those things? Because we know our Father. And we have absolutely no doubt that what He has said in His Word, He will faithfully do!

Grumble in the Lord Always

When Paul encountered difficult situations, instead of praying, "Oh Lord, have pity on me. Am I ever going to get out of this mess?" his declaration of faith was, "None of these things move me" (Acts 20:24). His bold confession was, *"Thanks be to God, who gives us the victory through our Lord Jesus Christ"* (1 Cor. 15:57 NKJV).

Just think about what was going on in Paul's life at the time he wrote some of his epistles. When he wrote the Book of Philippians, he was in jail. I remember when my husband and I visited the place where it is believed that Paul was in prison. It was more like a dungeon than a jail. As I stood there in that dungeon cell, I wondered how on earth Paul could write such an uplifting letter as the one he wrote to the Philippians when he was imprisoned in that awful place.

Just put yourself in Paul's situation for a moment. If you had been sitting there in that dungeon, what would you have said?

Most of us probably would have lost our joy very quickly. If we had been writing in our journals, we might have written the words, "Grumble in the Lord always, and again I say grumble." We would probably have forgotten all about what the Lord had said to us—that He would deliver us out of all our troubles.

And yet Paul, in the midst of that situation, wrote the words, *"Rejoice in the Lord always: and again I say, Rejoice"* (Phil. 4:4). He declared, *"I have learned, in whatsoever state I am, therewith to be content"* (Phil. 4:11). And he also wrote, *"My God shall supply all your need according to his riches in glory by Christ Jesus"* (Phil. 4:19).

When Paul said in Philippians 4:8, *"Whatsoever things are lovely, whatsoever things are of good report . . . ,"* his surroundings were not very lovely, and they certainly weren't good. But he still went on to proclaim, *". . . if there be any virtue, and if there be any praise, think on these things."*

Why could Paul say those kinds of things in the midst of the worst adversities anyone could ever imagine? Why did thanks and praise to the Lord continually come out of his mouth?

Paul's close, intimate relationship with his Heavenly Father gave him the confidence to believe that God was going to deliver him out of every circumstance that might come his way. He knew the ability and power of his Savior, and he constantly declared those things in the midst of his problems and struggles. And his bold declaration of faith was what activated God's mighty power!

When we have full confidence in our Heavenly Father, we can rejoice always. We can be content always. We can be fully persuaded that God will supply all of our needs according to His riches in glory by Christ Jesus.

Now I'm not saying that when you really know the Lord, you're not ever going to get discouraged. We're all human. We all encounter times of trouble and distress. We all face fear and discouragement.

Yet on the other hand, if we have a close, intimate relationship with our Heavenly Father, the Holy Spirit will be right there to encourage us, strengthen us, and deliver us. He will be our Healer, our Helper, our Provider, and the One Who meets all of our needs. We can pour out our discouragement and heartache to the Lord, and He will refresh us, give us an uplifting, encouraging word, and help us win a great victory!

God Will Bless Our Property Lines

People go through challenging times today just as they did in the Apostle Paul's day. Some have lost their jobs. Some have been struck by terrible symptoms in their bodies. Some have gone through horrendous attacks on their families or businesses.

It breaks my heart when I hear about people who know the Word of God and yet fall by the wayside when the turmoil and crises of life come. They simply don't know how to stand when trouble strikes because they haven't become intimately acquainted with their Heavenly Father.

But if they know their God as Paul knew Him, they will know that they can place their confidence in His Word and firmly stand their ground. And as they declare their faith in God's ability and power, they will find that He will deliver them out of every trial, every trouble, and every attack of the devil—because God takes care of His own!

I remember hearing a testimony from a farmer who lived in an area where there was a terrible drought. All the other farmers in his region were losing their crops.

But this particular man knew the Word of God. He had planted good seeds, and he was trusting the Lord for a good harvest. So he began to walk around his farm, declaring by faith, "My crops will prosper. There will be rain on my crops."

He reported later that when the rain came, it only rained on his property. The people around him just couldn't understand. The rain poured down all over his farm, but it stopped right at his property line. His crops were blessed and he had a great harvest when no one else did, because he knew his God and put his trust in Him. I'll tell you what—when we know our God and declare our faith in His Word, He is going to bless our property lines!

Declaring and Doing the Works of God

When Paul encountered a rough place—a test or trial—he didn't complain about the circumstances. Instead, he declared the power of God. Let's read in *The Message* Bible what he said concerning trials and tribulations.

2 CORINTHIANS 4:1, 17–18 (Message)

1 Since God has so generously let us in on what he is doing, we're not about to throw up our hands and walk off the job just because we run into occasional hard times.

17 These hard times are small potatoes compared to the coming good times, the lavish celebration prepared for us.

18 There's far more here than meets the eye. The things we see now are here today, gone tomorrow. But the things we can't see now will last forever.

Hallelujah! That's the kind of declaration we need to make—"These hard times are small potatoes compared to the good times that are coming." Paul was saying, "The best is yet to come!"

Then he went on to say that these problems and distresses that we sometimes encounter in life are only temporary. They're here today and gone tomorrow. The more we focus on the promises of God, the more we release His power to bring us out of those troubles.

But unless we know the Lord as Paul did, there's no way we can make that kind of bold declaration of our faith. There's no way we can have that kind of confidence in the Lord.

That's why our burning passion in life must *always* be to know our Heavenly Father more. Not to know Him to ask Him for something, but just to know Him—to know that He's there for us, that He is for us and not against us, that He's there to encourage us in times of discouragement, and that He will give us what we need at the specific time we need it.

Most important of all, we need to know our God so we can declare His wonderful works. The Apostle Paul dedicated his entire life to *declaring and doing* the works of the Father. And isn't that what Daniel was talking about when he said, "*The people that do know their God shall be strong, and do exploits*" (Dan. 11:32)? I'll tell you, this is what we were born for! This is the mission God wants us to accomplish here on this earth—to declare and do the works of the Father!

Are you ready to do mighty exploits for our God? Are you ready to declare the works of the Lord? May it be your prayer each day to connect with the Father's heart, to draw closer to Him than ever before—so you can declare His wonderful works and do mighty exploits for Him!

CHAPTER 4

Prayer Is the Air We Breathe

What is prayer? It's our divine connection with our Heavenly Father. It's that amazing gift that God has given us to communicate with Him. And prayer is the greatest privilege we have as Christians. It's such a privilege to pray! It's such a privilege for us to be able to talk to the Lord.

Not only is prayer a privilege, but it's absolutely vital for each one of us in our Christian walk. It is our life and our lifeline. It's the very thing that gives us strength.

J. Oswald Sanders once wrote, "[Prayer] is indeed the Christian's vital breath and native air."[3] I like to say it this way: "Prayer is to our spiritual life what oxygen is to our natural life." Or you could say, "Prayer is our spiritual oxygen."

While you've been reading this book, you've also been breathing in and breathing out. By the end of this day, you will have taken approximately 23,000 breaths. But when you woke up this morning, did you start counting your breaths—one, two, three . . . ? No, of course you didn't! Why not? Because breathing comes naturally to you. You don't even have to think about it.

We don't get up in the morning and say, "Okay, I have to take my oxygen for the day. Praise God, here's my one big breath of oxygen. That's all the oxygen I need for today." No.

What do we do? We breathe in and breathe out, breathe in and breathe out. We breathe in oxygen and we breathe out carbon dioxide. We do it naturally!

For a Christian, it should be the same way with our prayer life. Talking to God should be something we do automatically. It should be a normal thing for us to commune with our Heavenly Father. We should constantly breathe in the life of God and exhale all the stresses and struggles that try to infect our lives each day. We need to breathe in life and exhale all the hurts and disappointments that have come our way—and we need to do it daily!

When the enemy tells us, "You're not going to be able to balance your budget this month," we need to breathe in the prayer, "Oh Father, I thank You that all of my needs are met according to Your Word."

When the enemy whispers in our ears, "You're not going to get healed this time," we need to breathe in the prayer, "By the stripes of Jesus, I'm healed. I'm whole." We need to breathe in the promises of God!

Why do we get discouraged? Why do we get so frustrated and depressed and think we can't make it? Because we're not breathing in the oxygen of life that is prayer!

Prayer should be as natural to us as driving. When you first learn to drive, it's awkward. You have to think about turning the key in the ignition, putting your foot on the accelerator, and turning on the signal lights. But after you've driven a car for awhile, you don't have to stop and think, *Oh, I need to put my foot on the accelerator.* And you don't have to remind yourself every time you want to stop, *I need to take my foot off the accelerator and put it on the brake.* My goodness, if you had to think about all of that, you would probably have a wreck!

You do those things automatically. In fact, you're probably not even aware that you're doing them because driving has become so automatic to you.

That's the way God wants our prayer life to be. Our Heavenly Father wants us to develop such a strong prayer relationship with Him that prayer becomes an automatic response for us. If turmoil tries to come upon us or if we're being battered by the devil's attack, we're instantly going to pray. We're instantly going to take our authority in the Lord. And we're going to grasp the hand of our Savior and let Him bring us out on the other side of that problem even better than we were before!

Every time danger comes our way, it should be the most natural thing in the world for us to call upon the Name of our Savior. It should be our automatic response to talk to our Heavenly Father. And when we call upon the Lord and stand on His Word, we can expect Him to answer us!

What Is Prayer?

Prayer is the most powerful key that God has given us. It's the method He has designated for us to communicate with Him. Prayer is the one thing in life that we must not neglect, because it's the greatest opportunity we will ever have—the opportunity to talk to our Heavenly Father.

Prayer is not supposed to be something strange or weird. It's not something that we do only when we get ourselves worked up into a frenzy. Prayer is simply talking to our Heavenly Father just as we would talk to our earthly father.

Now you may not have a close relationship with your earthly father. In that case, you could also say that prayer is like talking to your best friend. It's so easy and natural to talk to your best friend. You can always tell your friend how you feel and ask for advice.

It's the same with your Heavenly Father. You can talk to Him freely because He *is* your Best Friend. He will always be there to listen to you, give you wisdom, and provide the answers you need. If you turn to your friends when you're troubled, they might be able to give you some good, uplifting advice. But your Heavenly Father will give you the *perfect* advice. It's so good to talk to the Lord!

There's an old song that says,

"Now let us have a little talk with Jesus.

Let us tell Him all about our troubles.

He will hear our faintest cry

And He will answer by and by.

Now when you feel a little prayer wheel turning,

Then you'll know a little fire is burning.

You will find a little talk with Jesus makes it right.

I may have doubts and fears,

my eyes be filled with tears,

but Jesus is a friend

who watches day and night;

I go to Him in prayer,

He knows my ev'ry care,

and just a little talk with Jesus makes it right."[4]

So many times when my heart has been heavy, I have gone to my Heavenly Father and poured out my heart to Him. I've cried out, "God, I don't understand," and I've told the Lord what was on my heart. And that's exactly what He wants us to do.

There is nothing like pouring out your heart to your Heavenly Father—talking to Him and allowing Him to talk to you. You don't have to go to the Lord with any big, fancy words. I think we sometimes wonder, *Am I supposed to pray eloquently and reverently to the Father, with all of these grand words?* But thank goodness, the Lord doesn't care what kind of words you use when you pray. He just wants you to talk to Him.

Sometimes I hear people praying in such pious voices and using all of these adjectives and adverbs when they talk to the Lord. They're saying things like, "Oh God, our most gracious Heavenly Father, the God of all the universe, the One Who made us." When I hear something like that, I think, *They must be praying to a stranger!*

When it comes to my conversations with my Heavenly Father, I talk to Him in common, everyday language. I talk to Him the same way I talked to my earthly father.

When I talk to the Lord, I get right to the point. I say, "Hey, God, this is what is going on in my life." And then I tell Him all about my troubles. Sometimes I remind Him, "God, You said if I would do this, You would help me and guide me."

When we develop the habit of talking to our Heavenly Father as if He's our Best Friend, it won't matter what struggles or rough places come our way—we'll instantly begin to pray and commune with Him. We'll instantly connect with Him. He will refresh us and restore us. He will renew our strength.

Thank goodness, He has a great big shoulder for us to lean on, and He just loves for us to pour out our hearts to Him!

Jesus Lived a Life of Prayer

Dwight L. Moody once said, "I would rather know how to pray . . . than to preach. . . ."[5] If you think about it, Jesus never taught his disciples how to preach. What did He do? He taught them how to pray (Matt. 6:9–15). Why did He teach them how to pray? Because He knew that prayer was the key to their success in life and ministry!

Prayer was always a top priority in the life of our Savior. He considered prayer more vital to His well-being than physical rest. When Jesus was here on this earth, He was in constant communion with the Father. We read in the Word that He often went aside and prayed (Luke 5:16 NIV). Even though He was extremely busy in His ministry, He never let that stop Him from taking the time to pray.

Now Jesus didn't talk to the Father because He had to. He had a strong desire—an overwhelming passion—to commune with His Father. He wanted to be united with the Father and empowered by Him!

What did Jesus do before He chose His 12 disciples—those who would work so closely with Him in the ministry? He talked to His Father. He prayed. Luke 6:12–13 says, *"Jesus went out to a mountainside to pray, and spent the night praying to God. When morning came, he called his disciples to him and chose twelve of them, whom he also designated apostles"* (NIV).

When Jesus' cousin, John the Baptist, was brutally executed by King Herod, what did the Lord do? He took time to withdraw to a solitary place where He could be alone with His Father (Matt. 14:13 NIV). Jesus was continually communing with the Father, praying to the Father, getting the Father's instructions, and letting the Father guide His steps.

If it was important for Jesus to pray, how much more important is it for us to pray? Jesus' whole life was one of dependence upon His Father and communion with Him. And that's how we should live—completely dependent upon our Heavenly Father.

Depending upon your Heavenly Father will keep you free from depression. It will keep you free from confusion and fear. When we encounter certain situations, we don't know what to do. But our Heavenly Father knows all the answers. If we're in communion with Him, He will lead us, guide us, and show us exactly how to handle them.

I depend upon my Heavenly Father every day of my life. Quite frankly, I'm not sure that I could get up in the morning if I didn't know that the Lord was so very close beside me. But since I'm certain that He is right there with me every moment of the day, I know I'm going to make it.

There may be some shaky ground that I must go over. There may be some rough spots in the road. But however bumpy or rocky the way, I know that my Heavenly Father is going to turn all things around for my good (Rom. 8:28). And that's the place we must get to—the place of total trust and dependence upon our God!

What is prayer? It's more than asking and receiving. It's more than presenting requests and waiting for answers. Prayer is a union with our Heavenly Father. It is our need pouring out and His grace pouring in. It is more than trying to force open a closed hand. Prayer is taking from an open hand. God is saying to us, "I've opened My hand to you. Now receive from Me."

Psalm 34:15 tells us, *"The eyes of the Lord are upon the righteous, and his ears are open unto their cry."* If you haven't been receiving from the Lord, perhaps you haven't been communing with Him. The Word says His ears are open to our cries. The Apostle Peter quotes these words in his first letter: *"For the eyes of the Lord are over the righteous, and his ears are open unto their prayers"* (1 Peter 3:12).

I can just see our Heavenly Father sitting on His throne right now, waiting for you to call upon Him in prayer. I can hear Him saying, "Sarah, I haven't heard from you lately," or "David, you haven't talked to Me in such a long time. My ears are open, but I haven't heard your cry."

Let me ask you a question. Are you talking to your Heavenly Father? Are you taking time to commune with the Lord? He desperately longs for you to call upon Him.

When you learn to commune with the Lord and allow Him to commune with you, there's a sweetness, a closeness, in your fellowship with Him. There's a feeling that you've just got to have Him by your side every moment of the day. As your soul cries out for your Heavenly Father, as your heart longs for Him, you will know that He is always there for you. And all you have to do when you need Him is call upon His Name!

CHAPTER 5

You Have Not Because You Ask Not

John Wesley once said, "God does nothing except in response to believing prayer."[6] That's the law He has designed to operate on this earth—the law of prayer.

In other words, our Heavenly Father works through the prayers of His people. He shapes the world by the prayers of His saints. But that means He has to find someone who will intercede in prayer.

If we want the will of God to be done on this earth, it is our responsibility to pray that His will is done. The Lord's Prayer says, *"Our Father which art in heaven, Hallowed be thy name. Thy kingdom come, THY WILL BE DONE in earth, as it is in heaven"* (Matt. 6:9–10). I don't know about you, but as long as I'm here on this earth, I want to be surrounded by the will of my Heavenly Father!

E.M. Bounds made the statement, "God shapes the world by prayer. The more praying there is in the world, the better the world will be and the mightier the forces against evil everywhere." He also declared, "The prayers of God's saints are the capital stock in heaven by which Christ carries on His great work upon the earth."[7]

Prayer is the responsibility of every Christian. God has called each and every one of us to pray. In fact, it seems that He cannot carry out His plan on the earth without the prayers of His saints, which means we have a mighty job to do in prayer!

The law of prayer requires us, as believers, to pray so God can answer our prayers. In other words, we are supposed to ask, and then He answers. Now, I know that God is all-knowing. Jesus said the Father already knows what we need before we ask (Matt. 6:32). He also knows our desires. But He still requires that we ask Him for those things. James 4:2 says, *"Ye have not, because ye ask not."* God expects us to ask!

Let me share a story with you that illustrates what I'm talking about here. When I was 16 years old, I had some babysitting jobs and was beginning to earn some money. At the time, contact lenses had just come out, and I desperately wanted to have some contacts. I had been wearing glasses, but now I desired to wear contacts.

I knew there was no money in our family's budget to provide contact lenses for me. So being the independent person that I've always been, I said to my dad, "I desire to have some contact lenses. I want to go to the bank and borrow the money for contacts."

My dad thought it was a good idea for me to establish some credit, even though this was certainly establishing credit at quite an early age. But my dad was not only a minister; he was also a businessman. And he thought this was a good thing for his daughter to do.

So he told me, "Okay. I'll go to the bank with you and you can borrow the money."

Before we went to the bank, I told my dad exactly what I wanted to do. Of course, I didn't know the banker myself, but my dad already had a relationship with him. I'm quite sure that he had probably made some kind of prearrangement with the banker that he would be responsible for the loan.

When we went into the banker's office, my dad and I sat down. Dad introduced me to the banker, and I thought surely he was going to explain what I wanted. But we just sat there for several minutes, and my dad didn't say a word!

Finally I thought, *If I'm going to get this loan, I'm going to have to ask for it myself.* So I gathered up my courage and said to the banker, "This is what I want to borrow. I have a babysitting job, and I'll pay it back."

"That's fine," the banker replied. Then I signed my name on the paper, and when we walked out of his office, I had the loan.

As we were leaving the building, I looked over at my dad and said to him, "Daddy! Why didn't you tell the banker what I wanted?"

My dad replied, "Lynette, I wasn't the one who wanted something. It was you. You needed to ask."

It's the same way in our relationship with our Heavenly Father. We can't depend on our spouses to ask God for the things we need. We can't depend on our friends to ask for us. And our children can't depend on us to ask the Heavenly Father for the things they desire. Yes, we can all lift each other up in prayer. But we all must learn how to ask the Father for ourselves!

Jesus Said to Ask

There are a number of passages in the Bible where the Lord Jesus Christ told us to ask. Let's read one of those passages from the Book of John.

JOHN 16:23–24

23 And in that day ye shall ask me nothing. Verily, verily, I say unto you, Whatsoever ye shall ask the Father in my name, he will give it you.

24 Hitherto have ye asked nothing in my name: ask, and ye shall receive, that your joy may be full.

Remember, when Jesus spoke those words, He was not addressing a crowd of world-renowned Christian televangelists. He was speaking to His disciples. He was speaking to you and me. He was speaking to each and every one of us who believes in Him. And He said that whatsoever we ask in His Name, the Father will give it to us. Jesus was urging us to *ask*!

In another passage from the Book of John, the Lord told His disciples, *"Whatsoever ye shall ask in my name, that will I do, that the Father may be glorified in the Son"* (John 14:13). After Jesus made that statement, the disciples must have looked at Him incredulously. They probably thought, *Jesus, are You talking about ANYTHING that we ask?*

So what did He do then? In the very next verse, He repeated what He had just said—*"If ye shall ask ANY THING in my name, I will do it"* (v. 14). But then He gave them the qualifier for their asking. Verse 15 says, *"If ye love me, keep my commandments."*

If you love Me! Jesus is talking about relationship, isn't He? You see, our asking is tied to our relationship with the Lord. It's tied to our love for Him and keeping His commandments. If we have a close, intimate relationship with Jesus Christ and we're obeying His commandments, *then* if we ask anything in His Name, He will do it for us.

The same thing is true in our natural relationships, isn't it? We're limited many times in what we can ask by how close we are to the person we're asking from. In other words, we can't just ask anybody for the "whatsoevers," can we?

If we don't have a close relationship with our Heavenly Father, it can be extremely awkward to go into the Throne Room and ask Him for something. We may feel that we need to have a "warm-up session," just to remind the Lord of who we are. But that's not the kind of relationship He desires to have with His children!

If you wonder why some people seem to receive more from the Lord than you do, perhaps they have a closer relationship with Him. If there seems to be a lack in your receiving from God, I encourage you to check up on how close you are to your Heavenly Father.

Are you continually communing with the Lord? Are you walking and talking with Him? Are you spending time with Him in prayer? Are you thanking Him for all that He's done for you? If you are, then He says, "*Whatsoever* you ask the Father in My Name, He will give it to you" (John 16:23). If we want to be able to freely ask our Heavenly Father for the things we need, it's so important for us to keep a close relationship with Him!

'That Your Joy May Be Full'

So many times when we think about asking God for something, we only consider our basic necessities. For example, if we need healing we know that the Word says, "*By whose* [Jesus'] *stripes ye were healed*" (1 Peter 2:24). So we ask God for healing and we receive from Him.

Or if we're struggling financially, we know that Philippians 4:19 says, *"My God shall supply all your need according to his riches in glory by Christ Jesus."* So we ask for God's provision and we receive the provision we need.

But God has so much more for us! Remember that Jesus said, *"Ask, and ye shall receive, THAT YOUR JOY MAY BE FULL"* (John 16:24). God is not only concerned about the big things—our health, our finances, and our families—but He is even interested in the little things that we desire, the "whatsoevers"!

Now your "whatsoevers" may not be the same as mine, because your desires are not necessarily the same as my desires. But one thing that's important to me with my busy schedule in the ministry is conserving time. And one way I can conserve time is to find a close parking place wherever I go.

You may think that sounds silly and trivial, but it's something that's important to me. So I always ask my Father for a close parking place!

Of course, sometimes my faith is tested in this area. You see, when I ask God for a close parking place, not only am I asking Him for something I desire, but I am exercising my faith. Thank God, He's always been faithful to give me a close parking place!

Another area where I've had many opportunities to exercise my faith is in praying about the weather. You see, we have a number of outdoor events associated with RHEMA Bible Church, and I don't want to have bad weather when we've scheduled such an event. For that reason, I started developing my faith in praying about the weather a number of years ago.

For example, each summer we host 30,000 to 40,000 people for a huge Fourth of July fireworks celebration called *Rockets Over RHEMA*. We have outdoor concerts with Christian bands, concession stands, and inflatable games for the children. It's a wonderful outreach to the community, and obviously we need the weather to cooperate.

For almost a week prior to one of our recent *Rockets Over RHEMA* events, weather forecasters predicted rain. I immediately began to pray and speak to that situation in the Name of Jesus, and I asked my Heavenly Father for good weather.

The day before the event, it absolutely poured. I told the Lord, "God, I don't care what the weather does today. But from noon tomorrow until midnight, I thank You for no rain."

The very night of *Rockets Over RHEMA*, a big storm was brewing in the west, and it was headed straight toward the RHEMA campus. I kept speaking to that storm in the Name of Jesus, and I also told the Lord, "Father, I don't care how You do it, but I thank You that it will not rain on this campus tonight as a testimony of Your faithfulness."

As the night progressed, I noticed on the local weather map that the storm was getting dangerously close. We had a Life Flight helicopter on campus for the event, and at 8:30 the pilot told one of our event coordinators, "I'm getting out of here. A bad storm is coming, and you need to disperse these people."

But the coordinator replied, "You don't understand our pastor's wife. She has a pact with God when she has events, and no storm is coming on this campus tonight!"

Then our coordinator, who is also a real promoter, told this pilot, "If the storm does not come, will you do an even bigger display for us next year than you've done this year?"

The pilot quickly replied, "You have my word on it. But I'm telling you, I won't have to do it because a storm is coming."

Around 9:15 I looked at the weather map again, and the storm was really bearing down on us. I thought, *Okay, God. I believe it's time for me to go inside and have a big conversation with You!*

So I went into the church building, into my prayer closet, and I said, "God, You and I have a pact that You will give me good weather for our outside activities."

Then I took authority over the devil, and I told him, "Satan, in the Name of Jesus, I command you to get out of here!"

Next I declared by faith, "Father, when You send good weather for this event, it's going to be a testimony to Your faithfulness, especially to those who have not accepted Jesus Christ as their personal Savior."

The next thing I knew, one of our church members who is a storm spotter came to me and said, "Lynette, I want to tell you what just happened. I was listening to my shortwave radio, and the reports said that a severe storm was about to hit Broken Arrow. All of a sudden they exclaimed, 'It's breaking up! It's breaking up!' Then, in the next few minutes, they officially declared, 'It's all clear for Broken Arrow.' "

As my husband and I were on our way home after the evening's events, we joined hands and thanked God for His faithfulness. What happened that night really spoke to me of our Heavenly Father's great love for us. He loves us so much that *whatever* we need or desire, He is right there to answer us!

I remember another time when my husband and I had an opportunity to exercise our faith concerning the weather. At this particular time we lived on a hill overlooking the city of Tulsa, and we had a lot of windows at the back of our house. That meant we had an excellent view of the weather, especially as the storm clouds rolled in from the west. And because we lived on a hill, there was absolutely nothing between us and the thunderclouds!

One evening a tornado hit Oklahoma City and was headed straight toward Tulsa. My husband and I were watching the weather reports on television when the weatherman suddenly urged viewers to "take shelter!"

Just at that instant the tornado sirens sounded in our neighborhood. We immediately began to declare, "No harm is going to come near us. We take authority over this tornado in the Name of Jesus." What were we doing? We were taking our authority in the Lord, but we were also *asking* our Heavenly Father for His protection.

Something strange happened to the tornado that night. When it reached the outskirts of the city, the entire storm suddenly split and went completely around Tulsa. I heard the weatherman exclaim, "I can't believe this storm just split. Somebody must have been praying." He actually said that on television!

Yes, we were praying. We were exercising our rights and authority in Christ. And we were asking our Heavenly Father to protect us. Our God will do some mighty and unusual things if we will but ask!

It's Time to Get Back to Our Childlike Faith

Oh, if we would only come to the Lord as a little child! When our children were younger, they would come to us and say, "Mother, Dad, would you do this for me? Would you get this for me? I'm hungry. I need something to eat. Would you help me?" And what did we do? We took care of their needs. We accommodated them.

Did you know that our Heavenly Father is right there to accommodate us too? He wants to be our great Provider. He wants to give us the things we need. He wants to give us wisdom. He wants to give us strength. He wants to open doors for us. And yet so many times, we're living far below our privileges *because we fail to ask.*

There's so much more to receiving from God than just confessing His Word and claiming His promises. Our Heavenly Father will move in a powerful way if we will just ask!

I believe it's time for us to revisit what God has already said to us. It's time for us to get back to that childlike faith—the faith we once knew in our hearts. We need to get back to a pure and simple faith in our Heavenly Father—as we ask Him for the things we need and receive the answers from Him!

CHAPTER 6

Stir It Up to Pray!

It's so wonderful when you make a strong connection with the Lord in prayer. It's so awesome when you're praying and all of a sudden a "gully washer" of prayer comes rushing up on the inside of you. You connect with the heart of God and move up higher in communing with Him.

Do you remember the fire of God that was ignited on the inside of you when you first received Jesus Christ as your Savior? It's so wonderful to feel that newness and freshness in your relationship with the Father. But God wants us to be stirred up in the Lord *every* day of our lives. He wants our hearts to continually cry out for Him in prayer!

I'm thankful that I've never lost the thrill of being with my Heavenly Father, worshipping Him, communing with Him, and learning more about His Word. We should never lose the thrill of our first love for the Lord. It's so important that we keep that flame burning in our hearts!

But if we want to keep that flame burning, we have to constantly stir up our passion for the Lord. If we don't stir up that excitement in our hearts for God, we'll lose our joy. We'll lose our sensitivity to the voice of the Holy Spirit. We'll lose our passion for the things of God. We must keep stirring ourselves up in the Lord!

I don't know about you, but I don't like dry praying. It's hard for me to pray when it's dry. If I'm struggling to pray, I feel like I'm not getting anywhere.

Besides, prayer should never be something dull—and it shouldn't be hard work. I want to enjoy every moment of my time in prayer. I want all of my prayers to be fervent. I want to be passionately moved to pray.

When I pray, I want to be surrounded by the presence of the Lord. I want to feel His presence so strongly. And when we continually surround ourselves with the presence of God, we can enter the Throne Room of the Father at any time.

I grew up in a Pentecostal denomination, and the Pentecostals knew what fervent prayer was. We prayed until we had "prayed through," as we called it—until we had "bombarded Heaven" and the anointing and power of God was felt in our midst. There is nothing like feeling the anointing and power of the Lord!

Of course, we know that we don't walk by sight and we certainly don't walk by our feelings. But it's good *to feel* God's power and anointing when we pray. And if we want to have that kind of fervency in our prayer life, we're going to have to stir ourselves up!

The Apostle Paul told Timothy, "*Therefore I remind you to stir up the gift of God which is in you through the laying on of my hands*" (2 Tim. 1:6 NKJV). The *Amplified Bible* says, "*That is why I would remind you to stir up (rekindle the embers of, fan the flame of, and keep burning) the [gracious] gift of God, [the inner fire] that is in you by means of the laying on of my hands.*" And remember what the Apostle Peter said in

Second Peter 1:13 (NKJV), *"I think it is right, as long as I am in this tent, to stir you up."*

Those verses remind me of something that happened when Ken and I were in Africa. We had a fireplace in our hotel room and it was the only heat we had. It happened to be cold at night, so the maid would come in and light the fire. Then she would take the bellows and fan the flame to get it roaring hot. That incident gave me a visual image of the way we need to stir ourselves up to pray.

You see, we are all called to pray. But we have to stir up the gift of prayer. And we need to keep stirring it up continually. Prayer is the bellows that blows upon the warm coals of revival and keeps the Body glowing with fervency.

I love to use the illustration of making a chocolate pie to help people understand what it means to stir ourselves up. You see, I have a chocolate pie recipe that my children dearly love. I make the crust from scratch. I make the filling from scratch. There's absolutely nothing instant about my chocolate pie!

I have all the ingredients for that chocolate pie in my kitchen at any given moment—eggs, milk, cocoa, flour, sugar, vanilla, and butter. But that chocolate pie is not manifested in my kitchen. Why? Because I haven't put the ingredients together.

Even if I put all the ingredients together, it wouldn't mean that I would have a chocolate pie. What would I have to do next? I would have to stir it up! When I make my chocolate pie, I have to stir and stir and keep on stirring, or the pie filling will stick and scorch as it cooks.

It takes time to stir that pudding until it's thick. But if I keep on stirring, I will have an awesome chocolate pie!

It's the same way with our prayer life. We have all the ingredients we need in order to have an awesome prayer life. But sometimes we neglect to "stir it up."

On the other hand, when we stir ourselves up to pray, we become totally engulfed in our prayers. We make a strong faith connection with the Lord. And that gives us more confidence that He is going to hear and answer our prayers!

Create an Atmosphere for Prayer

How do you stir yourself up to pray? How do you stir up a fervency in your prayer life? One of the keys that I have discovered and always endeavor to share is the importance of creating an atmosphere for prayer.

What do I mean by creating an atmosphere? Do you realize that every day people are creating atmospheres all around them? When you go to a sporting event, perhaps a football game, a certain atmosphere is being created. The band is playing "fight songs" and the team comes out on the field all pumped up. The atmosphere is charged with excitement about that ball game.

To create an atmosphere that causes you to desire to pray, you have to get your soulish realm opened up to the things of God so they can reach down into your spirit. And what do you think reaches more people in the soulish realm than almost anything else? Music.

Sometimes we don't realize how much music affects us. If we're in a room where fast-tempo music is playing, we may find ourselves tapping our toes to the music. On the other hand, if the music is slow, it may actually slow us down.

One of the best ways I know to create an atmosphere for prayer is through music. I'll tell you, good worship music can stir you up to pray and bring you into the very Throne Room of the Father!

A number of years ago, I began to use music to help me create an atmosphere for prayer. I started by surrounding myself with good Christian music 24 hours a day. Whether I'm at home, in my car, at our office, or in a hotel room when we travel, I play good, Word-based music to build me up all day and night.

If I awaken in the middle of the night, I immediately hear encouraging music playing—something that's going to edify and strengthen me—music that creates an atmosphere of worship and prayer to my Heavenly Father.

At night, the music is usually instrumental. But when I get up in the morning, I like to listen to someone singing songs that bring me into the very presence of God. Then it becomes so easy for me to pray. And I can start my day by praying fervently because my heart has already been opened up to the Lord.

Whether I'm sleeping, getting dressed in the mornings, driving my car, or working in my office, music brings me closer to the Lord. It keeps me surrounded with an atmosphere in which I can touch my Heavenly Father at any moment in prayer. And it opens up the windows of Heaven for me to hear from Him!

When I try to pray without music, I have such a dull time. I find myself praying simply because I'm being obedient to pray. But honestly, I don't believe as much is being accomplished during those times because I'm not passionately moved to pray. I pray so much more effectively when I do it with a God-given passion!

When I stir myself up to pray, I become so engulfed in my prayers that I sometimes miss my turn if I'm driving in my car. When I pray effectual, fervent prayers, by the time I finish praying, I'm completely charged up in the Lord!

I'll tell you, this kind of praying is what keeps me from getting stressed out in life. It's how I make the right decisions and avoid making mistakes. I stay in tune with my Heavenly Father by staying in an atmosphere of prayer!

Hungry for God

When you have a heart that is hungry for the Lord, it's so much easier to stir yourself up to pray. Matthew 5:6 says, *"Blessed are they which do hunger and thirst after righteousness: for they shall be filled."* And Psalm 107:9 tells us, *"For He satisfies the longing soul, And fills the hungry soul with goodness"* (NKJV). God desires for us to seek Him with a hungry heart. He wants us to be just as hungry to seek Him in prayer as we are to sit down and eat a piece of good chocolate pie!

I like to cook, but I have two rules when I cook. First, when I say the meal is ready, I want everyone to come to the table immediately. Second, I want them to come hungry.

You see, I pride myself on getting all the food ready at the same time, and when I set that food on the table, it's piping hot. I want my family and guests to eat the food when it's hot because that's when it has the best flavor. And I want them to come to the table hungry so they can eat the massive amount of food I've prepared for them.

One time my husband and children came to the table for dinner after I was already seated and eating my food while it was still hot. My husband told the kids, "Let's watch Mother eat while our food cools off enough for us to eat it." Somehow they didn't savor the food at quite as hot a temperature as I did!

Did you know that our Heavenly Father wants us to come to His table when the food is hot—when it's hot with His holy fire, so we will catch that fire and go out and perform the mission we were created for? He also wants us to come to Him hungry—hungry to hear from Him—hungry to receive His instructions. We need to hunger and thirst after the things of God. The hungrier we are for the Lord, the easier it's going to be to stir ourselves up to pray.

Jeremiah 29:13 says, "*You will seek me and find me when you seek me with all your heart*" (NIV). When we seek the Lord in prayer, it's so important that we seek Him with all of our hearts. It can't just be a form or ritual. It can't just be routine. Every prayer we pray should be fervent and heartfelt!

One Bible story that I love so much is that of Hannah. If you remember, Hannah desperately wanted to have a son, but she had never been able to have children (1 Sam. 1:2). So she went to the temple to seek the Lord in prayer.

When Hannah prayed, she was so moved in her soul by her desire to have a son that she sought the Lord with all of her heart.

1 SAMUEL 1:10–15 (Amplified)

10 And [Hannah] was in distress of soul, praying to the Lord and weeping bitterly.

11 She vowed, saying, O Lord of hosts, if You will indeed look on the affliction of Your handmaid and [earnestly] remember, and not forget Your handmaid but will give me a son, I will give him to the Lord all his life; no razor shall touch his head.

12 And as she continued praying before the Lord, Eli noticed her mouth.

13 Hannah was speaking in her heart; only her lips moved but her voice was not heard. So Eli thought she was drunk.

14 Eli said to her, How long will you be intoxicated? Put wine away from you.

15 But Hannah answered, No, my lord, I am a woman of a sorrowful spirit. I have drunk neither wine nor strong drink, but I was pouring out my soul before the Lord.

Hannah was stirred up to pray and she poured out her soul before the Lord. What was Eli's response?

1 SAMUEL 1:17 (Amplified)

17 Then Eli said, Go in peace, and may the God of Israel grant your petition which you have asked of Him.

God answered Hannah's fervent, heartfelt prayer, and she had a son whom she named Samuel. She faithfully kept her promise to give her son to the Lord. As soon as young Samuel was weaned, she took him to the temple and presented him to Eli. Let's read what she said to the prophet.

1 SAMUEL 1:27–28 (Amplified)

27 For this child I prayed, and the Lord has granted my petition made to Him.

28 Therefore I have given him to the Lord; as long as he lives he is given to the Lord. And they worshiped the Lord there.

Hannah's desire for a son was so strong that she didn't stop praying until her prayers were answered. And that's the way we need to be. We need to be fervent and passionate in our prayers. We need to seek the Lord with all of our hearts and pray so fervently that we refuse to stop praying until we receive the answer from Him!

Pray at All Times

When are we supposed to stir ourselves up to pray? Ephesians 6:18 tells us, *"Praying ALWAYS with all prayer and supplication in the Spirit, and watching thereunto with all perseverance and supplication for all saints."* The *Amplified Bible* says, *"Pray at all times."*

The Word of God has commanded us to pray at all times. And if it weren't possible for us to do that, the Lord wouldn't have told us to, would He? It's true that we live in a world where we are all scrambling for time. But in the midst of our busy lives, we must not let the enemy defeat us by stopping us from spending time in prayer.

I believe there are some very simple things you can do to help you pray at all times. If you'll put these things into practice, you'll find that you'll be in touch with your Heavenly Father continually. It will seem as if He's so close to you that you can draw upon Him at all times!

First of all, do you realize that you can do other things while you're praying? You can multitask in this area of your life, just as you probably multitask in other areas. I learned this from my father-in-law, the late Kenneth E. Hagin.

He would be engaged in a conversation with you, but while you were talking to him, it wasn't unusual to see his lips moving. He wasn't talking out loud. He was simply praying under his breath as he listened to you converse with him.

Sometimes this habit could make you feel as if he wasn't really listening. But he was. He simply knew the secret of keeping his spirit constantly in tune with the Lord by praying at all times.

I also remember seeing Brother Hagin watch television, and during the commercials he would pray. Or if he was watching a football game, he would pray in between the tackles. I mean, he would "help" the players run a touchdown, and the next thing you knew, he was praying very quietly, under his breath.

Sometimes people comment, "You mean Brother Hagin watched sports?" Brother Hagin loved sports! He was a man who loved life. In fact, one time he got so excited during a football game "helping" a runner make a touchdown that he flipped his recliner over. There he was, lying on the floor with his feet up in the air, moving his feet as if he could really help that runner run!

Over the years, I watched Brother Hagin's example of praying at all times, even during his normal daily activities, and it made me realize how important it is for us to stay in the Spirit and in an attitude of prayer. We need to surround ourselves with an atmosphere of prayer all the time.

Certainly there are times of concentrated prayer. There are times that we should fully devote to praying and seeking the face of God. But so often we get condemned if we decide to pray for an hour every day and then something happens and we don't get to spend a full hour. We can still pray at all times. We can still pray without ceasing.

Let me give you an example of how I start my day by praying at all times. First of all, I make my faith confessions. I begin by saying, "This is the day that the Lord has made. I will rejoice and be glad in it."

While I'm getting ready in the morning, I have various prayer stations—different places where I pray about certain things. I pray first about my family. I call each person's name in prayer, and then I say, "I thank You, Father, that every system in our bodies functions normally. Our blood functions normally. Every organ, every cell, and every nerve functions normally. We are all well, healthy, whole, and normal in every way. No evil shall overtake us. No plague shall come nigh us. With long life will You satisfy us and show us Your salvation."

Next I pray for the partners of our ministry. I thank God that He is blessing them abundantly—financially, emotionally, mentally, physically—in every way. I thank Him for giving them wisdom in whatever situation they may be going through—"Thank You, Father, that all wisdom does abound in them." Then I ask the Lord to bless their families and for His favor to be upon their lives.

At this point I begin to pray over my day. I ask the Lord, "What will I encounter today? Give me wisdom and strength.

Give me knowledge and favor. Give me the right connections and help me prepare for this day."

By the time I leave my house to go to work, I have already prayed for about an hour and a half. I've also been doing all the other things necessary for me to get ready in the morning. But while I'm doing those things, I'm communing with my Heavenly Father.

As soon as I get into my car, I put on my worship music to create an atmosphere of worshipping the Lord. As I drive to work, I fellowship with my Father. I spend time praising Him. I say, "Father, I love You so much. I thank You for Your goodness. You've been so good to me."

This is also when I ask the Lord, "Is there anything You want to talk to me about? Is there anything I need to do, any assignments from You for today?"

By the time I get to work, I'm in tune with the Lord. I'm in tune with His voice. And I'm ready for my day.

While I'm at work, I'm still listening to good Christian music. Although I'm handling the work I need to, I'm still communing with my Heavenly Father. No matter what I'm doing, I'm still meditating and praying. I'm keeping myself stirred up to pray!

I have been practicing this for many years, and it has helped me walk in peace, even when many big storms were raging around me. I have found such wonderful communion with my Heavenly Father, and praying at all times has become a natural thing to me!

Be Fervent and Passionate in Prayer

You may feel that you don't have time to pray. I understand that feeling. But when you create an atmosphere for prayer and stir yourself up to pray, you'll find yourself getting so excited about talking to God that it will be easy to pray at all times. I guarantee you, if you will practice the things I've shared with you in this chapter, it will revolutionize your life!

When you learn how to keep yourself in tune with your Heavenly Father 24 hours a day, it will bring you into a realm of communion with Him that you've never known before. It will open your heart up to the Lord. It will refresh you, renew your strength, and bring you so close to the Father that no matter what comes your way, you'll be able to draw the strength you need from Him.

So I encourage you to be fervent and passionate in your prayers. And stir yourself up to pray. The more you stir up the anointing and the boldness to pray, the more you'll see those things that you're believing for come to pass!

And when you reach the place where you feel that you just *have* to get down on your knees and touch Heaven, the heavens are literally going to be opened wide to you. Our Heavenly Father is calling for all of His children to stir ourselves up to be people of prayer!

CHAPTER 7

Prayer Is Your Power Plant

Did you know that your prayers are powerful? Your prayers are dynamite. Your prayers can move mountains. And they can dissipate every obstacle that stands in your way. Your prayers can help you climb out of the valley and get over on the mountaintop. There is so much power in prayer!

Prayer is the power plant of the Church. It is also the power plant of our lives. Prayer is the key that unlocks the vast treasures of Heaven's power!

Let's read a verse from James chapter 5 that describes how powerful our prayers are.

JAMES 5:16

16 The effectual fervent prayer of a righteous man availeth much.

JAMES 5:16 (NLT)

16 The earnest prayer of a righteous person has great power and produces wonderful results.

JAMES 5:16 (Amplified)

16 The earnest (heartfelt, continued) prayer of a righteous man makes tremendous power available [dynamic in its working].

Tremendous power is available to us as believers. But what must we do if we want to activate God's power? Pray! Time and again in the Bible, we are admonished to pray.

This verse in James chapter 5 is not talking about a trite, half-hearted, routine type of prayer. It's talking about earnest prayer. And earnest prayer is characterized by an intensely dedicated and serious state of mind. Earnest prayer is intense work!

The Power Plant

When you flip on a light switch, you expect the lights to come on, don't you? You expect to have electricity. Now I don't know all the mechanics of electrical power, but I do know that the light switches in our homes are connected to a breaker box. If that breaker box is not connected to a power source, you can flip the light switch all day long, but you still won't have any light.

The breaker box is connected to power lines, which in turn are connected to a power plant somewhere. The power plant generates the electricity that causes us to have lights in our homes.

Now let me ask you a thought-provoking question. If the electrical power in your home was generated from your prayer life, how bright would your lights be? Would they shine as brightly as they do when they're hooked up to the power plant at the electric company? Or would they be so dim that you would have to use a flashlight or light some candles to assist you? It's so important that we light our lives with the power of prayer!

I remember during the Christmas season several years ago, we experienced an ice storm in our area. Tree limbs were crashing onto the power lines, and all of a sudden, the lights in our home flashed off. In fact, the electricity was out in our entire neighborhood.

All of my appliances are electric so, of course, I couldn't cook. But at least I could turn on the gas fireplace. Worst of all, our water is supplied by an electric pump. Guess what? Not only did we have no lights, but we also had no water!

I didn't get too concerned for the first few hours, but after 24 hours without electricity, I began to realize how important electrical power really is. The next day was Christmas Eve, and I was planning to cook a big Christmas dinner for our family. So I began to pray fervently for those power lines to be repaired.

It was a massive job. The power company had to cut down trees and replace power poles. They told us that our power wouldn't be restored for at least 72 hours.

But my husband and I prayed, and when we came home from our Christmas Eve service at church, the lights at our house were back on. In fact, our whole neighborhood was completely lit up! I firmly believe the electricity in our neighborhood was restored because of the power of our prayers.

In years gone by, Christians were often driven to their knees in prayer just to survive the hardships of life. By comparison, we're living in relatively prosperous times. As a result, we don't often feel such an urgency to pray. And in many cases, we're not experiencing the power of God as Christians once did.

Many Christians today seem to be discouraged, despondent, and depressed. They wonder why their lives are falling apart—why things are happening the way they are. But the problem is, they have not stayed connected to their power source. And their power source is prayer!

I am convinced that so many Christians today are defeated because we haven't generated enough power from our prayer life. If we realized the awesome power of our prayers, we would pray more effectually. We would pray more fervently. And we would pray with more confidence that God will answer our prayers!

The Story of the 26 Armed Guards

I could tell you story after story about the awesome power that's generated through our prayers. But there's one particular story I want to share with you that I believe will help you understand just how powerful and effective *your* prayers are.

A missionary visiting his home church related the following incident that had happened while he was on the field. He said that while he was serving in a small field hospital in Africa, every two weeks he traveled by bicycle through the jungle to a nearby city for supplies. This was a two-day journey, and it required camping overnight in the jungle.

On one of these journeys, after he arrived in the city where he planned to purchase medicine and supplies, he observed two men fighting. One of them was seriously injured. The missionary treated his injuries and also witnessed to him about the Lord Jesus Christ. Then the missionary traveled the two days back through the jungle and arrived home without incident.

Two weeks later, he repeated the journey. Upon arriving in the city, he was approached by the young man he had treated a few weeks earlier. This young man told him the following story. "I was with some friends and we followed you into the jungle, knowing that you would camp overnight. We planned to kill you and take your money and drugs. But just as we were about to move into your camp, we saw that you were surrounded by 26 armed guards."

At this the missionary laughed and exclaimed, "Well, I was certainly alone out there in the jungle!"

But the young man pressed the point, saying, "No, sir. I was not the only person who saw the guards. My five friends also saw them and we all counted them. The reason we left you alone was because we were afraid of those guards."

At this point in the missionary's story, one of the men in the congregation jumped to his feet and asked the exact date this had happened. When the missionary told him, the man who had interrupted his story said, "On the night this incident occurred, it was morning here. I was preparing to go play golf. I was just about to leave the house when I felt the urge to pray. In fact, the urging from the Lord was so strong that I called several men in our church to meet with me here in the sanctuary to pray for you." Then the man added, "Would all of you men who met with me that day please stand up?"

One by one, the men stood to their feet. When the missionary had finished counting them all, guess how many there were? Twenty-six men—the twenty-six armed guards the young man and his friends had seen surrounding him in the jungle!

Oh, how powerful our prayers are! The time of prayer is a time of power. And we have an awesome, life-changing job to do for the Lord when we pray!

Tighten the Connection

Have you ever plugged in an appliance or a power tool and it didn't quite make the connection? Maybe the plug was a little loose and didn't stay in the socket. What happened? The tool would cut on and off, and it would leave you lurching from the power surges!

That's what happens in our lives sometimes. Perhaps we don't make a strong connection with our Heavenly Father. Or the connection isn't as tight as it should be. Sometimes we're on, sometimes we're off, and sometimes we're lurching from the power surges. Why? Because we haven't made a strong enough power connection through prayer!

Prayer is our divine connection with God. Prayer is tightening the connections with our Heavenly Father so that His power may flow freely to us, without loss or interruption. It's absolutely vital for us to stay plugged into God's power through prayer so we can keep ourselves built up in the Lord.

I've often heard people say, "I pray until I get a connection." You may not understand what that means, but those of us who have grown up in Pentecostal circles do. As I mentioned before, we called it "praying through." And I believe all of us need to tighten our prayer connection with the Lord until we "pray through."

It's so important for us to be united with our Heavenly Father. It's so important for us to be empowered by Him. The only way we can be united with and empowered by Him is through prayer.

When you plug your prayers into God's connection, what mighty power will explode through you! And if you stay plugged in tightly to the power of the Lord, when you call upon Him, He will say to you, "My child, what do you need? Do you need protection? Do you need healing? I'm ready to answer your prayer!"

Our Prayers Make Satan Tremble

Without prayer, you're going to be easy prey for the enemy. But prayer *is* the power that defeats the devil—any time, any place, no matter what the odds are. More dreadful blows are struck against Satan through prayer than we can possibly imagine. That's why he tries to keep us busy doing everything in the world besides praying—because he knows the awesome power of our prayers!

Do you realize that Satan is pulling out all of his tricks and strategies to use against the Church, because he knows his time is short? He's trying to take out every Christian he can. That's why it's so important for us to stand firm in the Lord and stay hooked up to His power. And the only way we can do that is through our prayers.

Let's read a passage from the Book of Ephesians that describes the power God has given us to overcome all the power of the enemy.

EPHESIANS 6:10–18 (NLT)

10 A final word: Be strong in the Lord and in his mighty power.

11 Put on all of God's armor so that you will be able to stand firm against all strategies of the devil.

12 For we are not fighting against flesh-and-blood enemies, but against evil rulers and authorities of the unseen world, against mighty powers in this dark world, and against evil spirits in the heavenly places.

13 Therefore, put on every piece of God's armor so you will be able to resist the enemy in the time of evil. Then after the battle you will still be standing firm.

14 Stand your ground, putting on the belt of truth and the body armor of God's righteousness.

15 For shoes, put on the peace that comes from the Good News so that you will be fully prepared.

16 In addition to all of these, hold up the shield of faith to stop the fiery arrows of the devil.

17 Put on salvation as your helmet, and take the sword of the Spirit, which is the word of God.

18 Pray in the Spirit at all times and on every occasion. Stay alert and be persistent in your prayers for all believers everywhere.

According to these verses we are going to encounter the powers of darkness. We are going to have to wrestle against spiritual wickedness in the unseen realm. But how do we overcome these things?

First, we put on the whole armor of God, not just part of the armor. And then in verse 18 it says, "Pray!" Prayer is the power that helps us overcome all the works of the devil. We have a responsibility to constantly, daily stand against the forces of evil through our prayers.

So don't pay any attention to the attacks and hindrances of the enemy. Stand firm in his face. Stand firm in confidence, keeping your prayer connection with the Father strong.

And stand together with your brothers and sisters in Christ. Remember, we're all fighting against the same devil, and we're fighting for the same mighty cause. Together, we can stand through any storm.

Prayer *is* the greatest weapon in our battle against the enemy. It's the most powerful tool in our entire arsenal. And prayer is the dynamic force that God has designed to help us stay connected to His mighty power.

Oh, if we could only grasp the importance of our prayer life! Without prayer, there is no power generated. Without prayer, we are defeated on every hand. It's time for us to crank up our prayer life and fervently seek the Lord—because prayer *is* the power plant of our lives!

CHAPTER 8

Pray, and Don't Faint!

Charles Spurgeon once said, "By perseverance the snail reached the ark."[8] Thank goodness he persisted until he got there!

The word *persistence* has been rolling around in my spirit recently, especially as it relates to our prayer life. Did you know that sometimes we have to be persistent in our prayers?

It seems in this day and age, if we encounter even the tiniest obstacle, we don't keep pressing on. We have a tendency to give up, go another route, or take a detour. But it's important for us to be persistent in our prayer life. It's time that we press into the promises of God!

The word *persistent* means "to go on resolutely or determinedly, or stubbornly, in spite of opposition." I also like this definition: "to remain unchanged or fixed."

As I was growing up, I was always a strong-willed child. I was extremely persistent, perhaps even to the point of being stubborn. My dad learned very quickly that he needed to channel my stubbornness and strong-willed nature and direct it toward the things of God. But that stubbornness, persistence, and strong-willed nature have helped me make it through many hard times in life.

I believe we can take our stubbornness and channel it into persistence, and we can make that persistence work for our good. We know that we need to be persistent if we want to accomplish anything in the natural. But we also need to be persistent if we want to accomplish anything for God. Above all, we need to be persistent in our prayers!

I had a precious aunt, my Aunt Oma, who was my mentor in prayer. Aunt Oma prayed loud, she prayed long, and she was persistent when she prayed. If you did not want your prayers to be answered, you had better not ask Aunt Oma to pray, because God always answered her prayers.

Sometimes I tell people that God answered Aunt Oma's prayers simply because he got tired of her communicating with Him about a certain issue. In other words, He got tired of her bugging Him. So He would answer her prayers, just to get her to stop bothering Him!

The Word says, "*Put me in remembrance*" (Isa. 43:26). Aunt Oma certainly believed in reminding the Lord on a consistent, daily basis of her needs and desires—whatever she was believing for.

I'm so thankful for the example I had in her dedicated, persistent prayer life. And I'm so thankful that as a young child, I learned how to be persistent in my prayers. I developed the attitude, "God, You can either answer my prayer fast or You can answer it 'long,' but I'm going to keep on praying until You answer." And that's the attitude we all need to have.

First Thessalonians 5:17 tells us, "*Pray without ceasing.*" That verse in the *Amplified Bible* says, "*Be unceasing in prayer [praying perseveringly].*"

When we present our requests to the Lord, there are times when we need to keep reminding Him of the things that we've prayed for. We need to say, "God, this is what You promised, and I'm going to keep reminding You of it until the answer is fully manifested." And we need to continually thank Him for the answer.

Yes, God heard us the first time we prayed. But sometimes we have to keep pressing in. Why? Because we're warring against the principalities and powers of darkness. We're wrestling against spiritual wickedness in heavenly places, against the powers of this dark world.

Do you remember what the angel said to Daniel when he prayed? Daniel had been in great distress, mourning for three weeks, and crying out to God in prayer. Suddenly an angel appeared to him and told him, *"Fear not, Daniel: for from the first day that thou didst set thine heart to understand, and to chasten thyself before thy God, thy words were heard, and I am come for thy words"* (Dan. 10:12). But then he added, *"The prince of the kingdom of Persia* [a satanic being] *withstood me one and twenty days: but, lo, Michael, one of the chief princes, came to help me"* (v. 13).

The Lord heard Daniel's prayer the instant he prayed. But there was a fight, a warfare in the heavenlies. It took 21 days for the angel of God to fight the principalities and powers of darkness and get through to Daniel with the answer to his prayer.

What if Daniel had given up and stopped praying? What if he had not persevered in prayer? Would he still have received the answer he was seeking?

We need to realize that there are prevailing spirits that are constantly coming against us—evil spirits that endeavor to harass us and block our prayers from being answered. And we must take authority over those things in the spirit realm and break their power!

Be Persistent in Prayer

In Luke chapter 18 Jesus told His disciples the story of a woman who took her case before an unjust judge. Then He exhorted them to *always* persevere in prayer.

LUKE 18:1–8 (Amplified)

1 Also [Jesus] told them a parable to the effect that they ought always to pray and not to turn coward (faint, lose heart, and give up).

2 He said, In a certain city there was a judge who neither reverenced and feared God nor respected or considered man.

3 And there was a widow in that city who kept coming to him and saying, Protect and defend and give me justice against my adversary.

4 And for a time he would not; but later he said to himself, Though I have neither reverence or fear for God nor respect or consideration for man,

5 Yet because this widow continues to bother me, I will defend and protect and avenge her, lest she give me intolerable annoyance and wear me out by her continual coming or at the last she come and rail on me or assault me or strangle me.

6 Then the Lord said, Listen to what the unjust judge says!

7 And will not [our just] God defend and protect and avenge His elect (His chosen ones), who cry to Him day and night? Will He defer them and delay help on their behalf?

> 8 I tell you, He will defend and protect and avenge them speedily. However, when the Son of Man comes, will He find [persistence in] faith on the earth?

Many years ago when personal computers first came out, our son, Craig, desperately wanted one. So he nagged me and nagged me until I finally told him, "Okay, Son, we'll get you a computer." Do you know why I bought him a computer? Because I wanted him to stop bothering me!

That's the way it was with this judge. He was an ungodly man, and yet because this woman kept asking him to give her justice against her adversary, he finally said, "Okay, I'll give you whatever you want!"

How much more does our Heavenly Father want to give us what we ask from Him? And we don't have to nag Him for it either! Jesus said in these verses from Luke chapter 18 that God will not only give us the things we ask for, but He will act speedily in our behalf!

At the end of this story, the Lord asked a pointed question: *"When the Son of Man comes, will He find [persistence in] faith on the earth?"*

Let me ask you a question today. When you pray, do you really believe God is going to give you the things you ask for? Do you expect to receive an answer from Him? Or do you get up from praying and say, "Okay, I've prayed, but if what I'm praying for doesn't happen, then I can do this and this"?

No! When we have faith in our Heavenly Father, whatever we ask, we should always expect it to happen. We must get to the place where we expect answers when we pray!

Don't Be Surprised When the Answer Comes

Let me give you another example of the importance of persistent prayer. There's an amazing story in Acts chapter 12 that describes what happened when prayer was made without ceasing for the Apostle Peter.

ACTS 12:1–5

1 Now about that time Herod the king stretched forth his hands to vex certain of the church.

2 And he killed James the brother of John with the sword.

3 And because he saw it pleased the Jews, he proceeded further to take Peter also. (Then were the days of unleavened bread.)

4 And when he had apprehended him, he put him in prison, and delivered him to four quaternions of soldiers to keep him; intending after Easter to bring him forth to the people.

5 Peter therefore was kept in prison: BUT PRAYER WAS MADE WITHOUT CEASING of the church unto God for him.

Notice that the believers prayed for Peter without ceasing. If you read further in this passage, you will discover that an angel came and rescued him from prison. He immediately went to the house where his fellow Christians had gathered to pray for him. But do you know what happened? When the chief apostle knocked on the door, they were so shocked to see him that they didn't believe it was really Peter!

A girl answered the door, and she ran back to tell the others, "Peter is here!"

But they thought she was mistaken. They told her, "No, you must have seen Peter's angel." She had a difficult time convincing them that it really was Peter, and yet that's exactly what they had been praying for!

We can learn a great lesson from this Bible story. We need to be persistent in our prayers and refuse to be in unbelief. And we shouldn't be surprised when God sends us the answers we're seeking from Him!

Lord, Send the Rain

Back in the early 1980s, Brother Hagin had an urgency in his spirit to gather together a group of believers at RHEMA Bible Training Center once a week to pray. In the building where we met, there were maps of all the countries of the world, and we prayed for God to send the rain of the Holy Spirit all across the earth.

He urged us every week to pray for "the precious fruit of the earth." Our foundational scriptures were Zechariah 10:1 and James 5:7.

ZECHARIAH 10:1

1 Ask ye of the Lord rain in the time of the latter rain; so the Lord shall make bright clouds, and give them showers of rain, to every one grass in the field.

JAMES 5:7

7 Be patient therefore, brethren, unto the coming of the Lord. Behold, the husbandman waiteth for the precious fruit of the earth, and hath long patience for it, until he receive the early and latter rain.

Brother Hagin would tell us, "Stretch your hand out and pray for whatever nation you feel led to pray for." And time and again, I would stretch out my hand and pray for Russia (the former Soviet Union).

When I was a little girl, people were building bomb shelters because we were so frightened of the atomic bomb. We were afraid the Russians were going to destroy us. I remember being terrified of Russia as a child, and that same fear stuck with me, even into adulthood.

When I first started praying for God to open a door to the Gospel in that part of the world, I merely prayed in hope. But as I persisted in prayer, my "hope prayer" gradually became a "faith prayer."

I didn't have any idea how the Iron Curtain could ever come down. But thank God, it came down! As we continued to pray, we saw the Berlin Wall come down and the Soviet Union collapse, and amazing doors were opened to take the Gospel throughout that region of the world.

But we didn't pray for just one week. We didn't pray for merely two or three weeks. We prayed every week, 52 weeks a year, for several years! We were persistent in our prayers. We did not give up. We did not get tired of praying. And God answered our prayers!

Don't Let the Devil Shake Your Faith

One of my favorite Bible stories that reveals the importance of persisting in prayer is found in Genesis chapter 32. It's the story of Jacob wrestling with the Lord.

If you remember, Jacob was a son of Isaac and Rebekah. He was Rebekah's favorite and his brother, Esau, was Isaac's favorite. Rebekah helped Jacob deceive his father into giving him the blessing that rightfully belonged to Esau. Of course, Esau was furious, and Jacob had to flee for his life.

So Rebekah sent Jacob to stay with her brother Laban. While Jacob worked for Laban, he began to learn the value of persistence. He fell in love with Laban's daughter Rachel, and he had to work for seven years to acquire her as his wife. But Laban tricked him and gave him Rachel's sister Leah instead. So Jacob had to work seven more years—a total of 14 years—for Rachel.

In the meantime, Jacob was very blessed. He had many children, servants, and large herds and flocks, as well as camels and donkeys. But Laban had not been fair with Jacob, so the Lord began to deal with Jacob that it was time for him to return to the land of his father, Isaac.

Jacob gathered his wives, children, servants, flocks, and all of his other possessions and began the long journey home. While he was on the way, he received word that Esau and 400 of his men were coming to meet him.

What did Jacob do? Naturally, he was terrified when he heard the news. After all, he had fled his own country because Esau was angry with him. Now his brother was coming to meet him with a whole army of men. He had no idea what Esau was going to do. Of course, he was afraid!

But, thank God, Jacob knew what to do when he was afraid. He cried out to God in prayer. Let's read more of his story.

GENESIS 32:9–12 (NIV)

9 Then Jacob prayed, "O God of my father Abraham, God of my father Isaac, O Lord, who said to me, 'Go back to your country and your relatives, and I will make you prosper,'

10 I am unworthy of all the kindness and faithfulness you have shown your servant. I had only my staff when I crossed this Jordan, but now I have become two groups.

11 Save me, I pray, from the hand of my brother Esau, for I am afraid he will come and attack me, and also the mothers with their children.

12 But you have said, 'I will surely make you prosper and will make your descendants like the sand of the sea, which cannot be counted.' "

Jacob was afraid, but he prayed to his God. And when we're struck with fear or apprehension, the most important thing we can do is pray and talk to our God.

After Jacob prayed, he devised a plan for meeting his brother. First, he divided the people who were with him into two groups, hoping that if one group was attacked, the other would escape. Then he sent some of his servants ahead of him with gifts from his herds and livestock to give to Esau, hoping to appease him. He repeated this several times while the company proceeded on their journey.

During the night, Jacob took his wives and children and went a little farther ahead. They came to a stream, and after his family had crossed over to the other side, Jacob stayed behind. It was there that he had an unusual experience with the Lord. Let's read this story from the *Amplified Bible*.

GENESIS 32:24–29 (Amplified)

24 And Jacob was left alone, and a Man wrestled with him until daybreak.

25 And when [the Man] saw that He did not prevail against [Jacob], He touched the hollow of his thigh; and Jacob's thigh was put out of joint as he wrestled with Him.

26 Then He said, Let Me go, for day is breaking. But [Jacob] said, I will not let You go unless You declare a blessing upon me.

27 [The Man] asked him, What is your name? And [in shock of realization, whispering] he said, Jacob [supplanter, schemer, trickster, swindler]!

28 And He said, Your name shall be called no more Jacob [supplanter], but Israel [contender with God]; for you have contended and have power with God and with men and have prevailed.

29 Then Jacob asked Him, Tell me, I pray You, what [in contrast] is Your name? But He said, Why is it that you ask My name? And [the Angel of God declared] a blessing on [Jacob] there.

Jacob was certainly persistent. He said, "God, I'm not going to let You go until You bless me." And he kept on wrestling until he received that blessing!

And that's what we need to do at times. We need to say, "God, I'm not going to let go of You until you bless me. I'm not going to give up until my prayer is answered. I'm not going to let go of Your promises."

Notice that the struggle did not shake Jacob's faith. So many times we're shaken in our faith when our prayers aren't answered instantly. But God doesn't want us to be shaken in our faith. He wants us to stand firm—to hold steadfast.

Jacob wasn't shaken in his faith, nor was he silent. He boldly declared, "I'm not going to let You go until You bless me!" Sometimes we need to have that kind of persistence with God. If you remember the rest of Jacob's story, his brother, Esau, wept when they saw each other again, and Jacob returned safely to his homeland.

When we have that kind of persistence in our prayer life, we won't be moved by circumstances. We won't be moved by the obstacles and hindrances in our way. Ephesians 6:13 says, *"Having done all, to stand."* When we stay steady in our faith as Jacob did, we will see the salvation of our God!

How Badly Do You Want It?

Sometimes I think God just wants to know how badly we want something when we pray. I'll tell you, if we let any little obstacle get in our way, we'll never make it in life. We'll never make it spiritually, and we'll never make it naturally either.

The blessings of God are not like ripe cherries falling off a tree! Receiving what you're seeking from the Lord requires hard work, preparation, and persistence. It takes toughness and tenacity, dedication and commitment. You have to press in until you receive the answer to your prayers, until you receive the victory.

So hold fast to the promises of God. And keep your eyes focused on the Lord Jesus Christ. Above all, be confident that what He has started through your prayers, He will perform until the answer comes!

CHAPTER 9

Prayer Impulses From Heaven

What do you think would have happened if we as Christians had been sensitive in our spirits to pray fervently and effectually before the 9/11 terrorist attack on America? Could we have averted that horrible disaster? I believe we could have.

It's so important, especially in these last days, that we not allow just the natural circumstances of life to stir our spirits up to pray. No! Our spirits should be stirred up to pray *before* events occur in the natural. We should learn to pray by the prompting of the Holy Spirit.

Many times we let our world dictate how we should pray. Outside forces strike at us and suddenly we're driven to our knees in prayer. But we really should be praying when the Holy Spirit triggers us *on the inside.*

When we allow the Holy Ghost to prompt us to pray, we can avert disasters, dissipate obstacles, and pull down strongholds in the spirit realm. As we respond to the Holy Spirit's promptings, He will give us wisdom and revelation. He will open doors of opportunity. He will propel us into His perfect plan!

It's Better to Pray on the Offense

Proverbs 20:27 says, "*The spirit of man is the candle of the Lord, searching all the inward parts of the belly.*" If we are sensitive in our spirits, the Holy Spirit will give us prayer impulses straight from Heaven. When we pray by the prompting of the Spirit, we can pray *offensive* prayers instead of always having to pray *defensive* prayers. It's so much better to pray on the offense than on the defense.

What do I mean by that? Defensive prayers are prayers that are triggered by the onslaught of the enemy. But offensive prayers are inspired by the promptings of the Holy Spirit.

When we pray defensive prayers, we're usually in the middle of a crisis and we're trying to play catch-up. We're desperately struggling to recover from the damage Satan has already inflicted on us. Let me give you a few examples of how much better it is when we pray offensive prayers.

Several years ago the home of one of the ministers in our area was struck by a devastating fire. The flames were so intense that the family almost didn't get all the children out of the house. But thank goodness, everyone escaped without serious harm.

About six months later, the home of another well-known minister in our area was destroyed by fire. The family was spared but the house was left in ruins.

After the second fire, I felt a prompting on the inside of me to pray. The Holy Spirit seemed to be warning me that this wasn't just a coincidence. It was the enemy trying to destroy the well-known ministers in this area. So I told my husband what I felt the Holy Spirit was saying to me, and we joined hands, took authority over the devil, and prayed that no harm would "come nigh our dwelling," according to Psalm 91. We exercised the rights and authority we have been given in the Name of Jesus.

A few months later our telephone rang in the middle of the night. It was the people who monitor our security system, and they told us, "Your smoke detector is going off."

At that moment, we could smell smoke, and it smelled like an electrical fire. Immediately the Lord brought to my remembrance that we had already prayed about this situation.

We quickly began to search the house, trying to find the source of the smoke, but we couldn't locate a fire anywhere. So I said to my husband, "Let's call the fire department."

"I'm not going to call the fire department until I find the fire," was his response.

"Honey, that's their responsibility," I pleaded with him. "Please call the fire department."

Even though I was putting my trust in my Heavenly Father to protect us, my mind was still going wild. So I grabbed my Bible and our wedding pictures, along with a few other things, just in case we had to evacuate the house!

Finally, we *did* call the fire department, and when they arrived they soon discovered the source of the smoke. A fan motor in one of our heating units had ignited and burned up. But even though the motor had burned up, no damage had been done to us or our home. Why? The devil's plans had been squashed because we had prayed by the prompting of the Spirit!

I remember another situation that occurred several years ago, during a time when my husband and son enjoyed riding motorcycles—dirt bikes. On one particular Saturday morning when they had planned to go riding, I awakened at 5:00 a.m.

I knew if I was wide awake at that hour of the morning, God must desire to talk to me, because I don't normally wake up that early. So I immediately began to pray.

As I prayed, I had this sickening feeling in my spirit. It was a feeling of impending danger for my husband and son. The feeling was so strong that it seemed as if the danger was all around me. I thought maybe the burden would lift as I prayed, but it didn't.

At first I was hesitant to say anything to my husband because I didn't want to spoil their day. But finally I told him, "Honey, I don't know what it is, but something on the inside is warning me that there is some kind of danger if you go riding today."

Thank goodness, Ken was sensitive to the Holy Spirit. He told Craig, "Son, we're not going today because your mom does not feel good about it."

Now you're probably wondering, "Well, what happened?" Nothing happened, because we listened to the Holy Spirit! My husband and son didn't step into an area where they would perhaps have been in danger, and we were spared from any type of accident or tragedy.

You see, if we're sensitive in prayer, if we'll listen to the Spirit of God when He prompts us in our spirits, He will show us the tricks and strategies the devil is trying to use against us. That's why we must stay tuned in to the Holy Ghost at all times!

How do we do that? How do we keep from being tripped up by the enemy? By meditating constantly in the Word. By communing with our Heavenly Father day and night. As we keep our spirits in tune with the Holy Spirit, He will warn us about things to come and alert us concerning other things we need to pray about.

The more you commune with the Lord and talk to Him, the more sensitive you'll become to His voice. His Spirit will begin to talk to your spirit and lead you and guide you as you pray.

Let me give you an example of what I'm talking about here. If someone comes to your mind, especially someone you haven't thought about for a long time, don't just think, *Oh, I wonder how so-and-so is doing?* That person is not coming to you by accident. The Holy Spirit is trying to prompt you to pray for that person. You may not know exactly what they're going through, but God does. And He wants you to pick up on His signal and stir yourself up to pray!

When I am prompted by the Holy Spirit to pray, I first pray about everything I know to pray about, and if the urgency to pray is still there, I begin praying in the Spirit. I allow the Holy Ghost to intercede through me and pray whatever He needs to pray.

I've heard testimony after testimony about people who have been awakened in the night with a burden to pray. They would find out later that someone on the other side of the world was in danger, and they were praying and interceding at that exact time!

Don't underestimate the promptings of the Holy Spirit to pray. If you're suddenly awakened in the middle of the night, don't assume it must have been the pizza you ate for dinner. Don't just roll over and go back to sleep! Someone may be in danger. That may be the prompting of the Holy Ghost, trying to stir you up to pray.

You may never find out what disasters you have averted or what blessings you have helped bring to pass through your prayers. But it's so important for you to listen when the Lord is stirring you to pray—because the most important prayer you can ever pray is the one inspired by the Spirit of God!

Read the Warning Signs

So often in life there are warning signs from the Holy Spirit all along our way, but we haven't fine-tuned our spirits enough to recognize those warnings. Let me give you an example of what I'm talking about here.

Years ago when I was single, I didn't know that a car had to be tuned up from time to time. I didn't realize the oil needed to be changed every so often. In fact, I was so ignorant about a car that I didn't even recognize the warning signs—the noises the car was making—that might be saying, "Hey, I need help!" But after paying a few repair bills, I learned.

My brother-in-law was able to do some mechanic work, and I remember telling him one time, "When I put my foot on the brake, it makes this funny noise. It sounds like something is grinding."

After he drove my car, he exclaimed, "You have no brake pads left!" Of course, I'm sure there had been warning signs all along, but I hadn't fine-tuned myself enough to recognize them. So I encountered a crisis situation with my car that could have been avoided if I had been sensitive to the warning signs.

That same kind of thing happens to us in our prayer life. God is trying to warn us about the devil's plots and strategies. The Holy Spirit is trying to stir us up to pray. But we're so inexperienced at hearing His voice that He can't get our attention until a crisis suddenly strikes.

Or we're so busy trying to put out a fire over here and a fire over there that we don't have time to pray in those areas where the Holy Spirit is urging us to pray. If we would only listen when the Holy Spirit warns us in our spirits and pray ahead of time, we wouldn't have to spend so much time putting out those fires!

Are You Endued With Power From on High?

It's so wonderful to pray by the unction of the Holy Ghost. It's so important for our spirits to be hooked up with God's Spirit when we pray. Romans 8:26 says, *"Likewise the Spirit also helpeth our infirmities: for we know not what we should pray for as we ought: but the Spirit itself maketh intercession for us with groanings which cannot be uttered."*

Jesus told His disciples to wait in Jerusalem until the Comforter—the Holy Spirit—came (Acts 1:4). On the Day of Pentecost, the Holy Ghost came, just as Jesus had promised. And when the Holy Ghost came, when the One Who would endue them with power from on high came, they began to speak in other languages—languages they did not know.

Sometimes the Holy Spirit may prompt us to pray in a heavenly language. At other times He may prompt us to speak in a language we don't know personally but that is still known to man.

I remember one time when I was visiting some of our church members who were in the hospital, I prayed for a woman who was about to go into surgery. It was a very serious situation, and this woman was extremely fearful. She was Hispanic, and I do not speak Spanish. But as I prayed for her that day, I began to pray in tongues. When I had finished praying, she asked me, "Lynette, did you know that you were speaking in Spanish?"

"No," I replied. "I don't know any Spanish."

"It was such a confirmation and a comfort to me," she continued. "You were saying in Spanish, 'All is well. All is well.' "

Thank God, as we open up our hearts to the Lord, the Holy Spirit will pray through us the very thing that needs to be prayed! (To learn more about praying in the Holy Spirit, I encourage you to read the minibook *Why Tongues* by Kenneth E. Hagin.)

Pray According to the Will of God

Romans 8:27 tells us, *"He that searcheth the hearts knoweth what is the mind of the Spirit, because he maketh intercession for the saints ACCORDING TO THE WILL OF GOD."* When we pray with our own human understanding, we may find ourselves praying according to our own will. But when we pray in the Spirit and by the promptings of the Spirit, we will pray according to the will of God.

I remember many years ago when Patsy Cameneti was over the prayer groups who prayed for our ministry and RHEMA Bible Training Center. She would meet with them and tell them what we wanted them to pray about.

One particular group prayed specifically for my husband. He was operating in the office of evangelist at the time and traveling heavily in crusades. So Patsy told this group to pray that the heart of the evangelist would be manifested more strongly in him.

As they began to pray, the Holy Ghost started bringing different things to them to pray about. Suddenly they found themselves praying, "Thank You, Lord, for giving Ken Jr. a pastor's heart." That's what was coming to them by the Spirit.

So they told Patsy, "We want to obey you, but every time we start to pray, we wind up praying for a pastor's heart."

"Oh, no, no!" Patsy exclaimed. "That's not his gifting. Go back in there and pray for him to have an evangelist's heart."

So they would go back and begin to pray again, but as soon as they started flowing with the Holy Spirit, all of a sudden they were prompted to pray, "Lord, thank You for giving him a pastor's heart."

This went on for quite a while, and each time they reported back to Patsy, she would say, "No, you've got it all wrong! I'm sorry, but that's not what you're supposed to be praying." Of course, they didn't want to be disobedient, but the same thing kept coming to them by the Spirit every time they prayed.

Finally, Patsy decided there must be something to this. So she said to them, "Don't tell anybody what you're praying about. Do not tell a soul on this campus. But whatever comes up in your spirits, go ahead and pray it out."

Of course, Ken and I didn't know anything about what those prayer warriors were praying, and they were true to their word. They did not tell a soul what they were praying about.

In June of the same year, the Lord started dealing with my husband about pastoring. Suddenly a pastor's heart was being birthed in him. Finally, he came to me and said, "Honey, the Lord is dealing with me about starting a church."

Now he had no idea what my reaction to that would be. For many years I had believed that God had called us to be pastors. But at this particular point, I was happy being in the traveling ministry. Even so, I was thrilled that I had actually been right about our calling to be pastors!

In October of the same year, we held our first service at RHEMA Bible Church, and we have already celebrated our 25th anniversary! It's been an exciting time in the Lord. But I'm so thankful for those pray-ers who were sensitive to the Holy Spirit and prayed for my husband to have a pastor's heart!

If We Only Knew the Power We Possess

We're living in a dangerous world today. Up until 9/11, most of us felt that America was a relatively safe place to live—a far safer place than any other country on earth. Then, all of a sudden, the enemy invaded our peaceful land.

Who would ever have thought that our personal safety would be threatened as much as it has been in recent years? So often fear threatens our minds because there's so much havoc in the world around us. But I firmly believe that as we stay sensitive in our spirits, the Lord will protect us and keep us out of trouble. He will help us avoid the traps of the devil. He will alert us to impending danger. And He will warn us concerning things to come. It's absolutely vital in these last days for us to be sensitive to the Spirit of God!

In this hour the enemy is using any means he can to trick us, get us on the wrong road, and even destroy us. But when we're sensitive to the things of the Spirit, we can prevent those tragedies in the spirit world and avoid situations that are intended for our harm.

Besides, the Holy Spirit is so far ahead of everything this world has to offer. The direction and wisdom He gives are far beyond anything we could ever receive from the world. That's why it's so important for us not to override what He's saying in our hearts!

So I encourage you to keep your ears open to the heart of God and get ready to receive those prayer impulses from Heaven. Oh, if we only knew the power we possess when we pray by the prompting of the Spirit! We must learn to walk in that power, walk in that strength, walk in that boldness, and walk in that knowledge. We must stay tuned in to the Spirit of God and be sensitive to His promptings at all times!

CHAPTER 10

Why Our Prayers Are Hindered

Have you ever wondered why some things you have asked the Lord for have not come to pass? Many times we get discouraged or disillusioned when it seems as if our prayers aren't being answered. The devil starts whispering in our ears, "See! God is not performing what He's promised in His Word." And sometimes we even begin to question the Lord.

I always remember my father-in-law saying, "If I'm not receiving from God, I don't check up on His end because I know that His promises are true and He does not fail. I check up on my end as to why I'm not receiving." So if it seems as if you're hitting a brick wall when you pray, I encourage you to check up on yourself and find out why!

First of all, you can ask yourself, "Am I following the rules of the house?" What do I mean by that? As you were growing up, you probably had rules at your house, didn't you? You had curfew times. You had certain instructions you had to follow.

I know as I was growing up, if I followed my parents' rules, I reaped the rewards, the benefits. I was blessed. I received favor. Why? Because I was following the rules of the house. But if I broke those rules, the wrath of my dad came upon me, and sometimes the wrath of my mother, which was worse! So I learned at an early age that if I wanted the blessings to come upon me, I'd better follow the rules.

It's the same in our relationship with our Heavenly Father. He has set down certain statutes and principles in His Word, and He tells us, "If you do this, I'm obligated to do this." But if we want to experience His blessings, we have to hold up our end of the bargain!

Let's look for a moment at what the Bible says about this subject in Deuteronomy chapter 28.

DEUTERONOMY 28:1–8

1 And it shall come to pass, if thou shalt hearken diligently unto the voice of the Lord thy God, to observe and to do all his commandments which I command thee this day, that the Lord thy God will set thee on high above all nations of the earth:

2 And all these blessings shall come on thee, and overtake thee, if thou shalt hearken unto the voice of the Lord thy God.

3 Blessed shalt thou be in the city, and blessed shalt thou be in the field.

4 Blessed shall be the fruit of thy body, and the fruit of thy ground, and the fruit of thy cattle, the increase of thy kine, and the flocks of thy sheep.

5 Blessed shall be thy basket and thy store.

6 Blessed shalt thou be when thou comest in, and blessed shalt thou be when thou goest out.

7 The Lord shall cause thine enemies that rise up against thee to be smitten before thy face: they shall come out against thee one way, and flee before thee seven ways.

8 The Lord shall command the blessing upon thee in thy storehouses, and in all that thou settest thine hand unto; and he shall bless thee in the land which the Lord thy God giveth thee.

What does the Word say? If we hearken (or listen) diligently to the voice of our God and obey His commandments, we will be blessed—blessed in the city, blessed in the field, blessed coming in, and blessed going out. All of our enemies will fall down before us.

But if you read a little further in that same chapter, you'll find out what happens if we *don't* hearken to the voice of the Lord our God and obey His commandments. The blessings will not come upon us, will they? We cannot prosper as God desires if we don't obey His Word!

Rules for Receiving the Blessings

If we want to experience God's blessings in a certain area of our lives, we need to find out what the rules are for receiving those blessings. For example, if we're praying for God's protection, Psalm 91 gives us wonderful promises for that.

It says that our Heavenly Father will be our refuge and our fortress. He will deliver us from the snare of the fowler, from the pestilence, from the terror by night, and from the arrow by day. He will deliver us from all types of destruction. But what are the rules for receiving God's protection? Verse 1 says that we must dwell in the secret place of the Most High. We must abide in the shadow (or shelter) of the Almighty. In other words, we must draw near to God. That's when we will experience His protection!

Or perhaps we're praying for the Lord to bless us financially. I've watched people claim the promise in Philippians 4:19—*"My God shall supply all your need according to his riches in glory by Christ Jesus"*—but they're not giving one penny to the Lord. And yet the Bible teaches us that we must give *first* if we want to be blessed. Jesus Himself said, *"Give, and it shall be given unto you"* (Luke 6:38).

We see this same principle in Malachi chapter 3.

MALACHI 3:10

10 Bring ye all the tithes into the storehouse, that there may be meat in mine house, and prove me now herewith, saith the Lord of hosts, if I will not open you the windows of heaven, and pour you out a blessing, that there shall not be room enough to receive it.

Here the Lord told His people to bring their tithe *first*, and *then* He would open the windows of Heaven. We would be amazed at how much we would prosper financially if we would only obey the commands of the Lord!

Sometimes I've heard people pray for God to help them overcome the temptations of the devil. They claim the promise in James 4:7—*"Resist the devil, and he will flee from you."* But what does the first part of that verse say? *"Submit yourselves therefore to God."* If we would learn how to submit our entire will to the Lord, I believe we would find it much easier to resist the devil's attacks!

Of course, anytime we're praying for our needs to be met, one of the most important scriptures we must always obey is Matthew 6:33—*"Seek ye first the kingdom of God, and his righteousness; and all these things* [that you need] *shall be added unto you."* It's so important for us to obey God's rules. When we do, He will prove Himself faithful to His Word every time!

Beware of Pride

Do you remember how prideful the Pharisees were? They were always telling others how good they were and saying things like, "I thank the Lord that I'm not like this poor tax collector" (Luke 18:11). But the Word tells us that their prayers were in vain because they lifted themselves up. (See v. 14.)

The most important thing we can do as Christians is to keep a humble spirit. James says, *"Draw nigh to God, and he will draw nigh to you.... Humble yourselves in the sight of the Lord, and he shall lift you up"* (James 4:8, 10).

Certainly God wants us to be confident about who we are in Christ. But we are to lift up the Lord, not ourselves. As these verses tell us, if we humble ourselves before God, He will lift us up! Besides, it's not what *we* can do; it's what *He* can do through us—through a willing vessel.

Another reason why our prayers are sometimes hindered is found in James 4:11. It says, *"Do not speak evil of one another, brethren. He who speaks evil of a brother and judges his brother, speaks evil of the law and judges the law. But if you judge the law, you are not a doer of the law but a judge"* (NKJV).

It's absolutely vital that we do not judge one another. There is one Lawgiver Who is able to save and destroy, and He alone is the Judge. Jesus Himself said, *"Judge not, that ye be not judged"* (Matt. 7:1).

One of the biggest problems we have when we begin to judge others is that we try to categorize sins. For example, on a scale of one to 10, we might say that sins in category one—perhaps jealousy or strife—are not so bad. We think it's okay for us to be jealous of our brethren. But sins in category 10—such as adultery or lust—are "big." Those are the sins we believe we can't be forgiven for.

According to our categories, it's okay for us to stir up strife, because that sin is only at category one on our scale. But it's really *not* okay, is it? What does the Word say about strife?

PROVERBS 6:16–19

16 These six things doth the Lord hate: yea, seven are an abomination unto him:

17 A proud look, a lying tongue, and hands that shed innocent blood,

18 An heart that deviseth wicked imaginations, feet that be swift in running to mischief,

19 A false witness that speaketh lies, AND HE THAT SOWETH DISCORD AMONG BRETHREN.

That's talking about strife, isn't it? So often we ignore strife and discord as if it's okay, and yet I've seen churches totally destroyed because of discord that's been sown among the brethren.

Sin cannot be categorized from one to ten. Sin is sin, regardless of what it is. But I'm so thankful that our Heavenly Father has made provision for us if we do sin. First John 1:9 says, *"If we confess our sins, he is faithful and just to forgive us our sins, and to cleanse us from all unrighteousness."* And Jeremiah 31:34 tells us that God will not remember our sins!

When I look at Jesus' ministry, I don't find condemnation or a judgmental attitude. He always lifted people up. He always forgave people. And He admonished us to forgive.

The Word says, *"Blessed are the merciful: for they shall obtain mercy"* (Matt. 5:7).

God had mercy on us, didn't He? Our ancestors, Adam and Eve, messed up royally. They doomed us all. What if God had said, "Why should I save mankind? Why should I give them a second chance? They got what they deserved"? He could have said that. But what did He do? He loved us so much that He gave the very best Gift He had—His precious Son, the Lord Jesus Christ—to redeem us.

God has been merciful to us, so it's important for us to be merciful to others and not judge each other. It's important for us to learn how to forgive.

Of course, Jesus knew this would be difficult for us. That's why He admonished us to love our enemies.

LUKE 6:35–38

35 But love ye your enemies, and do good, and lend, hoping for nothing again; and your reward shall be great, and ye shall be the children of the Highest: for he is kind unto the unthankful and to the evil.

36 Be ye therefore merciful, as your Father also is merciful.

37 Judge not, and ye shall not be judged: condemn not, and ye shall not be condemned: forgive, and ye shall be forgiven:

38 Give, and it shall be given unto you; good measure, pressed down, and shaken together, and running over, shall men give into your bosom.

Notice in these verses that right after Jesus talked about the importance of forgiveness, He talked about our giving—*"Give, and it shall be given unto you."* In other words, Jesus ties our forgiveness to our giving and also to our receiving from the Lord. It's so important for us to forgive, because unforgiveness affects every area of our lives!

Your Faith Won't Work Unless You Forgive

We always have such a strong desire to appropriate the great faith scriptures, especially Mark 11:23–24. Let's read those verses right now, even though you may already know them by heart.

MARK 11:23–24

23 For verily I say unto you, That whosoever shall say unto this mountain, Be thou removed, and be thou cast into the sea; and shall not doubt in his heart, but shall believe that those things which he saith shall come to pass; he shall have whatsoever he saith.

24 Therefore I say unto you, What things soever ye desire, when ye pray, believe that ye receive them, and ye shall have them.

What do we usually do when we read those verses? We get so excited. We exclaim, "Whatever I believe in my heart and confess with my mouth, I'm going to possess. Bless God, I claim this, I claim that, and I believe I have it, in the Name of Jesus!" But we tend to completely overlook the next two verses.

MARK 11:25–26

25 And when ye stand praying, forgive, if ye have ought against any: that your Father also which is in heaven may forgive you your trespasses.

26 But if ye do not forgive, neither will your Father which is in heaven forgive your trespasses.

I remember when my father-in-law taught on these scriptures. I heard him say over and over again, "Your faith is not going to work unless you forgive." I don't know about you, but I want my faith to work. I don't want anything to hinder my relationship with my Heavenly Father. So I have learned to forgive and forget!

I am amazed at how many people in the Body of Christ today are so easily offended and continually hold offences in their hearts. Many Christians have harbored a grudge for years. They say they have forgiven, but they have not forgotten. And if they haven't forgotten, they haven't really forgiven, have they? Why do I say that? Because one of the definitions of the word *forgive* is "to cease to feel resentment against (an offender)."[9]

According to that definition, if we still feel resentment toward someone, we haven't truly forgiven that person. And if there's unforgiveness in our hearts, our prayers are going to be hindered.

Now if you don't think you're going to be tested in this area, let me tell you, you will be! The devil has many people out there that he can use, and there is nothing he loves better than to send those people across your path.

I've had plenty of opportunities to forgive in my life, so I'm not telling you anything I haven't had to practice myself. You see, it's always been difficult for me to forget the hurtful things people have done to me. I would think that I had forgiven them, but in the back of my mind, I would still remember the hurt. So I began to pray for God to give me spiritual amnesia anytime someone hurt me. I told the Lord, "I want the hurtful things to go in one ear and out the other, never to be remembered anymore."

I decided that no matter what anybody said about me or how someone hurt me, I was going to do what the Lord Jesus Christ did when He hung on the cross. I was going to say, *"Father, forgive them; for they know not what they do"* (Luke 23:34).

Even though it's been many years since I made the decision to forgive and forget, the very first scripture that I read every day is Matthew 5:44—*"Love your enemies, bless them that curse you, do good to them that hate you, and pray for them which despitefully use you, and persecute you."* In fact, my Bible automatically flips open to that verse!

You see, I have to keep my flesh under just as you do. I have to remind myself each day that I have made a decision to bless people and not curse them. Why? Because I don't want my prayers to be hindered!

I was finally able to get to the place where I could love the people who had hurt me. I could bless them and forgive them, and I might even be able to forget what they had done to me. But to pray for them! I wanted to pray for them, all right. I wanted to pray that the wrath of God would come upon them. But we can't do that.

What has the Word commanded us to do? To love one another (John 15:12). It's sad that in the Christian world today we sometimes spend more time trying to destroy each other than we do forgiving and restoring each other. It's a shame that rather than showing brotherly love, so often we kill our wounded.

Galatians 6:1 tells us that when someone has been overtaken in a fault or has fallen into sin, God wants us to restore that person. He wants us to lift up and encourage that person, and take that one under our "wings of protection."

What did Jesus say to the woman who was caught in the act of adultery? " '*Neither do I condemn you; go and sin no more*' " (John 8:11 NKJV). When we're confronted with those kinds of situations, so often we wrap our righteous robes around us and say, "What an awful sin that person committed. I would never do anything like that." But when we make those kinds of statements, we're setting ourselves up for a fall.

How much better would it be if we would learn to exercise the God-kind of love—a love which forgives, forgets, brings in the wounded, and says, "I want to love and restore you"? First Peter 4:8 tells us, *"And above all things have fervent charity among yourselves: for charity* [or love] *shall cover the multitude of sins."* You see, love is a shield. When you love somebody, you're going to forgive them, aren't you?

Until you conquer loving your enemies and those who do terrible things to you, you're going to have opportunity after opportunity to practice forgiveness. But the more you learn to walk in love, the easier it's going to be for you to forgive the wrongs that are done to you.

Why does the Word of God speak so much about loving? Because it's the hardest thing in the world for us to do. In all honesty, the person that we love the most is ourselves. The Word does tell us to love ourselves. But Galatians 5:14 also says, *"For all the law is fulfilled in one word, even in this; Thou shalt love thy neighbour as thyself."* And if you love your neighbor as yourself, you won't have any trouble forgiving them and doing what's best for them, will you? You'll be able to put *their* needs first!

Draw Near to the Lord

If you want your prayers to be answered, you must draw near to the Lord. You must draw close to Him. Open your heart to receive from your Heavenly Father. And as you do, He's going to reveal the things that are hindering your prayers.

You wonder why you're not being blessed—why you're not prospering. You wonder why God's Word is not coming to pass in your life. It could be because you're not obeying His rules—His Word.

Or perhaps you're faithfully confessing the Word, but nothing seems to be happening. You don't understand why your faith is not working. It might be because you are not walking in love. What does faith do? It "*worketh by love*" (Gal. 5:6).

Or you may be harboring bitterness in your heart. I believe the Lord is saying to you right now, "If you will get rid of that bitterness and make an adjustment in your heart, those things that have been troubling you will turn around for your good."

If you have unforgiveness in your heart toward anyone, I encourage you this very moment to ask the Lord to forgive you. Then go ahead and forgive that person, no matter what they did to you. Just make a quality decision, "Yes, it was wrong. No, I didn't deserve what they did to me. But I'm going to forgive them and let it all go."

Sometimes we just need to have a good, honest reality check. It's so important for us to let the Lord deal with our hearts! As we listen closely to the voice of the Holy Spirit, we need to check up on ourselves and begin to search our own hearts.

Remember, the spirit is willing, but the flesh is weak. We are constantly warring against the flesh. There may not be any actual sin in our lives, but what are the weights, the things that are holding us back and keeping us from being close to the Lord? Those are some of the things that can hinder our prayers and prevent them from being answered.

Above all, let's endeavor to stay humble and not judge others. Let's overlook the shortcomings of those around us and look at the positive things about them. And let's do our best to lift them up.

If we want our prayers to be answered, if we want God to hear us when we pray, we must make a decision to practice the love walk—to walk down the love path. Remember, love is always the best way!

CHAPTER 11

Two Can Put Ten Thousand to Flight

The theme song of today's world seems to be "It's All About Me." People are always clamoring to know, "What can gratify me? What can make me happy? What is this going to do for me?" And if it's not going to do anything for them, they're probably not going to participate in it.

Paul talked about this kind of attitude in Second Timothy 3:1–2, 4 when he said, *"This know also, that in the last days perilous times shall come. For men shall be lovers of their own selves . . . Traitors, heady, highminded, lovers of pleasures more than lovers of God."*

Unfortunately, the attitudes described in those verses have crept into the church world today. But in order for God to accomplish what He wants in these last days, His people are going to have to lay aside those selfish attitudes and come into agreement in prayer. When all of God's saints join together and pray, His mission on this earth will be accomplished!

But what does the enemy so often use against us? Division! He knows how powerful our agreement is, so he tries to divide us so we won't be able to have an effective attack on him. It's a trick of the enemy to try to scatter and divide, because he knows if he can scatter the children of God, he can thwart the plan of God.

What did Jesus say about the power of agreement?

MATTHEW 18:18–20

18 Verily I say unto you, Whatsoever ye shall bind on earth shall be bound in heaven: and whatsoever ye shall loose on earth shall be loosed in heaven.

19 Again I say unto you, That if two of you shall agree on earth as touching any thing that they shall ask, it shall be done for them of my Father which is in heaven.

20 For where two or three are gathered together in my name, there am I in the midst of them.

When two or three believers are gathered in Jesus' Name, He said that He would be in the midst of us. And the Lord also declared that if two of us agree on earth as touching *anything* we ask, it shall be done for us!

Let's read this passage from *The Message* Bible.

MATTHEW 18:18–20 (Message)

18 "Take this most seriously: A yes on earth is yes in heaven; a no on earth is no in heaven. What you say to one another is eternal. I mean this.

19 When two of you get together on anything at all on earth and make a prayer of it, my Father in heaven goes into action.

20 And when two or three of you are together because of me, you can be sure that I'll be there."

I really like that! Jesus said when believers get together and agree upon anything, our Father in Heaven goes into action.

These verses from Matthew chapter 18 are more than just a promise from the Lord. *They are the plan that God has established for the Church!*

You see, Heaven is waiting for earth to get into agreement—for Christians to get into agreement. God wants all of His children to come together in unity. When we come into agreement and join together in one accord, it moves us into a different realm—into another power level of prayer!

There's so much more power in two than in one. We don't merely have twice as much power when we come into agreement. Our agreement moves us from the realm of addition to the realm of multiplication. We have multiplied power when we agree together in prayer!

DEUTERONOMY 32:30

30 How should one chase a thousand, and two put ten thousand to flight . . . ?

LEVITICUS 26:8

8 And five of you shall chase an hundred, and an hundred of you shall put ten thousand to flight: and your enemies shall fall before you by the sword.

That verse says all of our enemies will fall before us! When we move from praying alone to praying corporately, we move into a realm which produces dynamic results.

Even in the natural, powerful things happen—powerful successes—when people come into agreement. We can see this principle in Genesis chapter 11—the story of the Tower of Babel.

GENESIS 11:1–6 (NIV)

1 Now the whole world had one language and a common speech.

2 As men moved eastward, they found a plain in Shinar and settled there.

3 They said to each other, "Come, let's make bricks and bake them thoroughly." They used brick instead of stone, and tar for mortar.

4 Then they said, "Come, let us build ourselves a city, with a tower that reaches to the heavens, so that we may make a name for ourselves and not be scattered over the face of the whole earth."

5 But the Lord came down to see the city and the tower that the men were building.

6 The Lord said, "If as one people speaking the same language they have begun to do this, then nothing they plan to do will be impossible for them."

Notice that the Lord said, "Nothing they plan to do will be impossible for them." I don't believe He made that statement simply because they all were speaking the same language. They also had come into unity of purpose. They were of one mind and one accord.

Of course, the Tower of Babel was not the will of God. The Lord had to intervene in that situation and confuse the people's language so He could keep them from accomplishing their goal. But this story illustrates so clearly that nothing will be impossible for us, as the Body of Christ, when we come together in unity and harmony!

Jesus Prayed for Us to Become One

Let's look at Acts chapter 1 and see what happened when Jesus told His followers to come together according to the will of God.

ACTS 1:4–5 (NIV)

4 On one occasion, while he was eating with them, he gave them this command: "Do not leave Jerusalem, but wait for the gift my Father promised, which you have heard me speak about.

5 For John baptized with water, but in a few days you will be baptized with the Holy Spirit."

Jesus said to His disciples, "I want you to go into Jerusalem and wait there for the promise of the Holy Ghost." But what if the disciples had not obeyed? What if they had decided not to come into unity and one accord and wait for the Holy Spirit as Jesus had told them to do?

If the disciples had not come into unity and one accord, Jesus' mission on this earth would have failed. But thank God, they obeyed the Lord. They came together with one purpose and one goal—to wait for what had been promised to them by the Lord.

ACTS 2:1–4

1 And when the day of Pentecost was fully come, they were all with one accord in one place.

2 And suddenly there came a sound from heaven as of a rushing mighty wind, and it filled all the house where they were sitting.

3 And there appeared unto them cloven tongues like as of fire, and it sat upon each of them.

4 And they were all filled with the Holy Ghost, and began to speak with other tongues, as the Spirit gave them utterance.

Because the disciples obeyed the Lord and came into agreement—into one accord—Christ's mission on this earth succeeded!

Do you realize what a great responsibility we have as Christians? If we do not do what God has called us to do, His mission on earth will fail. Remember, Heaven is waiting right now for earth to come into agreement.

Besides, one of the great goals that the Lord Jesus Christ has for the Church, His Body, is for us to be in agreement. In John chapter 17, He prayed that we would become one.

JOHN 17:20–22 (NKJV)

20 "I do not pray for these alone, but also for those who will believe in Me through their word;

21 that they all may be one, as You, Father, are in Me, and I in You; that they also may be one in Us, that the world may believe that You sent Me.

22 And the glory which You gave Me I have given them, that they may be one just as We are one."

Let's read verse 21 again from *The Message* Bible:

JOHN 17:21 (Message)

21 The goal is for all of them to become one heart and mind—Just as you, Father, are in me and I in you, So they might be one heart and mind with us. Then the world might believe that you, in fact, sent me.

Jesus is saying, "Father, I want not only My disciples to become one and come into agreement, but also everyone they win to Me. I pray that all of them may be one as You and I are one." And as believers everywhere become one, great power, great manifestations, will occur!

A Symphony of Prayer

Let's look at Matthew 18:19 a little more closely.

MATTHEW 18:19

19 Again I say unto you, That if two of you shall agree on earth as touching any thing that they shall ask, it shall be done for them of my Father which is in heaven.

The Greek word that Jesus used for *agree* in this verse is suggestive of our English word *symphony*.[10] I believe Jesus was speaking in these verses of a symphony of prayer.

In a symphony orchestra, the instruments vary and the musicians don't all play the same parts. They play many different notes, and yet all the notes are in harmony with each other.

Of course, if you happen to be in the audience when an orchestra is warming up, it's not really music to your ears, is it? The musicians are not in harmony. They're not playing the notes on the score. Instead, they're playing whatever notes they want to play in order to warm up.

Sometimes that seems to be what is happening in the Christian world today. We're all just playing whatever notes we want to instead of playing the score God has set before us. And it is *not* music to anyone's ears.

But when it's performance time and the orchestra is warmed up, the conductor raises his baton and the musicians start to play. Although they're not all playing the same note, they're in harmony. They're in unity. And the performance is beautiful.

When we as Christians come into agreement in prayer, we may pray a little differently from each other. I may be the tenor saxophone with a melodious sound, while you may play the trumpet part and sound the charge. We don't all play the same parts, but as we come together in a symphony of prayer, it produces powerful results. And as we all play the notes on the score God has set before us, it creates a beautiful sound for everyone to hear!

There Is Strength in Bundles

Isn't it wonderful to have people who will stand with you in prayer? When we bind together in one mind and one accord, strengthening each other, encouraging each other, and holding each other up, what great heights we're going to reach for the Lord.

I believe in these last days God is creating spiritual connections for each of us with people who will agree with us in prayer. We need to lift each other up now more than ever before—because the enemy's attacks are so strong. There are times when we just need somebody to stand with us in faith!

Did you know that there is strength in bundles? What do I mean by that? You can easily break one stick, but if you put together a bundle of sticks, it's almost impossible to break that bundle. That's because there is so much strength in unity!

I remember many times when my precious Aunt Oma would call and say to me, "Lynette, I want you to agree with me about something," and we would agree together in prayer. One particular time, my dad was in the hospital. He had lost a lot of blood, but the doctors couldn't find the source of the bleeding.

So Aunt Oma said to me, "Lynette, agree with me that the source of that blood is going to dry up, the bleeding is going to stop, and he is going to be fine."

"Aunt Oma, I agree with you," I replied, and then we prayed for my dad.

Every day she would call me—sometimes twice a day—and ask, "Lynette, have you been praying?"

"Yes, Aunt Oma, I've been praying."

During that time, the doctors checked every organ of my dad's body. They performed test after test and the reports showed that everything was perfect. However, when they checked his stomach, they suddenly discovered the source of the bleeding. There was one little drop of dried blood in the area of his stomach. That was all that was left of the blood flow that had caused him so much trouble!

Remember, Aunt Oma had asked me to agree that the blood flow would dry up. And it did. There is so much power when we agree together in prayer!

I remember another time when my husband and I first started traveling with Kenneth Hagin Ministries. We were driving through the mountains of Colorado in a motor home, when all of a sudden Ken noticed that the gas gauge was on empty.

It was getting dark and we were way out in the middle of nowhere. Every service station we passed for miles was closed, and we were only getting four miles to the gallon, at the most. To top things off, we had our two small children with us. I mean, this was a desperate situation!

So we joined hands and agreed together in prayer. We said, "God, no matter how far we have to go, this vehicle will take us there. Our fuel will last until we find a service station that's open." We drove at least 75 or 100 miles that night before we finally found a service station that was open. But our fuel miraculously lasted all the way to that station. Thank goodness there is so much power when we agree together in prayer!

Revival Is Always Preceded by Prayer

I believe it's more important than ever for Christians to be united in prayer, because it's prayer that is going to bring about this last, great-day revival. You see, revival is always preceded by prayer.

The great revival that swept America in 1857 and 1858 began with one man who invited others to pray with him at noon in a church in New York City. At the time these prayer meetings occurred, the United States was experiencing financial panic. Banks were failing. Factories were closing. Unemployment was increasing. Does that sound like anything we've experienced in the economy in recent years? But the financial panic in that day triggered a religious awakening.

Gradually, the crowds at the prayer meetings increased. As the news reached outlying cities, other prayer groups sprang up. After six months, 10,000 businessmen were meeting daily at noon in New York City alone—all because one man had invited people to pray for revival.

It's estimated that of the total U.S. population of 30 million at the time, at least one million came to Christ in a two-year period. That's nationwide revival, isn't it? And it all began with one man and one city starting a prayer meeting for revival.[11]

I'll tell you, I have never been so excited in all of my life, because I believe the Lord is preparing His people today for revival. We're already entering into the last, great-day revival. And those revival fires are going to be fanned into flame as all the saints of God get down on our knees and fervently pray.

You see, revival is fueled by prayer. It's fired by God's Spirit. It's ignited with His glory. And this revival is going to be the most glorious ever experienced in the history of the world.

Can you see how important it is for us to come into agreement, to unite in prayer with the believers around us? When we do, great things are going to happen—we're going to be a mighty force for God!

Are you ready for revival? Are you ready to get down on your knees and pray? When the people of God come into unity and one accord, it brings a powerful response from the Father. And as we stay united in prayer and faith—there is nothing, absolutely nothing, that can stop us!

CHAPTER 12

Watchmen on the Walls

"And I sought a man among them who should build up the wall and stand in the gap before Me for the land. . . ."
—Ezekiel 22:30 (Amplified)

The Lord is searching this land for men and women who will build up the wall and stand in the gap for our nation. God is searching for His people who will combine the powerful principles of His Word and the power of prayer on behalf of our land.

One of the most important positions we must take in these last days is the position of praying for our country. Our country desperately needs prayer. God desires for us to earnestly and faithfully beseech Him on behalf of our great nation.

How important is it, then, for us as believers to be watchmen on the walls of our nation—watchmen who will pray day and night so we can live peaceful and godly lives, as the Word promises us (1 Tim. 2:1–2)? I don't want the Lord to say that He looked for a man, for a woman, to stand in the gap for the United States of America and found none.

That's why I'm asking you today to stir yourself up and join me in praying for America. I believe it's time for all of

God's people to join together and pray. You see, it's the prayers of the saints that will keep this country safe from harm and determine its destiny in this hour!

A Firm Foundation

I believe we live in the greatest country on earth. But our land is far from perfect. In fact, we have strayed so far from the biblical principles our nation was founded upon that we are in a sad condition right now.

You see, this nation was founded on the words *One nation under God.* America was an answer to prayer for people who wanted to worship the Lord freely. There was great expectancy as many people from the European nations traveled the waves of the Atlantic to come to a land with freedom of religion.

The Baptists, Quakers, Roman Catholics, Methodists, Presbyterians, Mennonites, Lutherans, Puritans, and many others came. Their goal was to find a place where they could worship God in Spirit and in truth. I'm sure the Lord was pleased by these people who wanted to put Him first in their hearts, as well as in their national affairs.

America's first president, George Washington, inserted the words *so help me God* into the oath of office for the presidency at his first inauguration.[12] At a meeting of the Provincial Congress in 1774, Washington, John Adams, Patrick Henry, and many other well-known leaders knelt before the Lord, seeking His blessings on America.

Years later, when the members of the Constitutional Convention spent many days arguing about the organization and wording of America's Constitution, 81-year-old Benjamin

Franklin reminded the delegates of those prayers that had previously gone forth. Although he was so ill that he had to be carried into the conference hall, Franklin nevertheless managed to stand and deliver these words:

> "In the beginning of the Contest with G. Britain, when we were sensible of danger we had daily prayer in this room for the divine protection. Our prayers, Sir, were heard, and they were graciously answered. . . . Have we now forgotten that powerful friend? I have lived, Sir, a long time, and the longer I live, the more convincing proofs I see of this truth—that God governs in the affairs of men. And if a sparrow cannot fall to the ground without his notice, is it probable that an empire can rise without his aid? We have been assured, Sir, in the sacred writings, that 'except the Lord build the House they labour in vain that build it.' I firmly believe this; and I also believe that without his concurring aid we shall succeed in this political building no better than the Builders of Babel. . . .
>
> "I therefore beg leave to move, that henceforth prayers imploring the assistance of Heaven, and its blessings on our deliberations, be held in this Assembly every morning before we proceed to business, and that one or more of the Clergy of the City be requested to officiate in that service."[13]

Franklin openly recognized that God does "govern in the affairs of men," and he urged his fellow delegates to make time to pray as they had done in the past. Many delegates—led by Washington—did gather for a July Fourth sermon followed by morning prayers. And eventually, Franklin's suggestions were implemented. Two chaplains were appointed—one to the House and one to the Senate—to invoke God's blessings before all sessions.

Notably, the Constitution these delegates finally agreed upon is the same one we're using today. It was written over 200 years ago, and our nation is still being governed by it. I firmly believe the reason we're still able to use that Constitution is because it was bathed in prayer.

Prayer! What would happen if our present Congress spent time in prayer and fasting before every session? What would happen if we, as believers, would all fast and pray for our country?

We need to realize that the Bible *is* the cornerstone of our society. Just as Jesus Christ paid a price on the cross for our spiritual freedom, our forefathers paid a price for our natural freedom.

Our country was founded upon God—not on any other god, but upon the Lord God Jehovah. Even our coins say, "In God We Trust." It's absolutely vital for us to carry this principle to the next generation. We must not keep silent, but we must pray day and night until this nation returns to the biblical principles upon which it was founded!

Earnest and Disciplined Prayers

First Peter 4:7 tells us, "*The end of all things is at hand: be ye therefore sober, and watch unto prayer.*" The *New Living Translation* of that verse says, "*The end of the world is coming soon. Therefore, be EARNEST AND DISCIPLINED in your prayers.*"

As I mentioned in a previous chapter, the Lord has declared that in these last days perilous times will come. But He has also instructed us to be *earnest and disciplined* in our prayers. I believe the time has come for us to take our place in praying fervently for our country.

Unfortunately, we concentrate so often on praying for our own needs that we forget we have a greater commission—to be about Kingdom business. And that includes praying for our great land!

It's so easy for us to complain about the problems in our nation and the privileges we no longer have. But if we would take our place in prayer and stand in the gap, the Bible says that our land would be healed.

2 CHRONICLES 7:14–15

14 If my people, which are called by my name, shall humble themselves, and pray, and seek my face, and turn from their wicked ways; then will I hear from heaven, and will forgive their sin, and will heal their land.

15 Now mine eyes shall be open, and mine ears attent unto the prayer that is made in this place.

God says if we will humble ourselves and pray, He will heal our land. Oh, how our land needs to be healed! We are living in critical days, and I believe it's only the prayers of the saints that will keep our nation on the right course.

Notice what Second Chronicles 7:15 says in the *New Living Translation*: *"My eyes will be open and my ears attentive to every prayer made in this place."* Thank God, the Lord is tuned in to our prayers. He is always listening! Our Heavenly Father hears *every* prayer we make.

If that is true, some may ask, then why aren't more good things happening on this earth? Perhaps it's because we have not been praying as we should. The Bible says that when we pray, God goes into action. How vital it is that we begin to pray for our nation. And we must not wait for a tragedy to occur before we pray!

Unfortunately, it seems that it often takes a crisis to bring us to our knees in prayer. That's exactly what happened after the 9/11 terrorist attack on America. It was so easy to call a prayer meeting after that terrible disaster. People flocked to church, united and inspired to pray because of what the devil had triggered against us. Even the Democrats and Republicans forgot about party lines as they stood together with hands joined to recite the Pledge of Allegiance. They loudly declared that America is "One nation under God."

Sadly, this unity and all the fervent prayers that went forth didn't last. Americans quickly returned to their daily routines—to business as usual.

I don't know about you, but I'm not willing to go back to business as usual! I'm not willing to sit back and let our country face an attack of that magnitude ever again. We should have been praying as fervently for our country *before* 9/11 as we did *afterward*. But we had grown comfortable and complacent in our prayers.

We must stay on guard and pray offensively for the safety of our land. When we do, I believe that whatever plots have been formed against the United States of America are going to be averted as our intelligence agencies are alerted and guided by the Spirit of God.

The enemy is always looking for an opportunity to knock us down. But the Word promises us that when we pray, no plan of the enemy will succeed.

PSALM 21:11 (NKJV)

11 For they intended evil against You; They devised a plot which they are not able to perform.

PSALM 21:11 (Amplified)

11 For they planned evil against You; they conceived a mischievous plot which they are not able to perform.

Now that's a scripture you can stand on when you pray for the safety of our country!

Job 5:12 also tells us that the Lord "*frustrates the devices of the crafty*" (NKJV). Praise God, when we bow our heads and pray, no weapon that's formed against our nation will prosper (Isa. 54:17)!

Praying for Those in Authority

It is our responsibility to stand in the gap, to build a hedge of protection around our country. But where do we begin? Let's look at the instructions Paul gives us in First Timothy chapter 2.

1 TIMOTHY 2:1–2

1 I exhort therefore, that, first of all, supplications, prayers, intercessions, and giving of thanks, be made for all men;

2 For kings, and for all that are in authority; that we may lead a quiet and peaceable life in all godliness and honesty.

In his letters, Paul encouraged Timothy on a number of subjects. He encouraged him to fight the good fight of faith (1 Tim. 6:12), watch his life and doctrine closely (1 Tim. 4:16 NIV), and stir up the gift of God inside him (2 Tim. 1:6), just to name a few. But Paul exhorts Timothy here, "Your most important assignment is to pray."

The Word admonishes us in these verses that *first of all*, supplications, prayers, intercessions, and giving of thanks be made for all men. Specifically, we are to pray for kings—or for our president—and all others who are in authority. The *Amplified Bible* says in verse 2 to pray "*for kings and all who are in positions of authority or high responsibility.*"

I like what it says in *The Living Bible*:

1 TIMOTHY 2:1–2 (TLB)

1 Here are my directions: Pray much for others; plead for God's mercy upon them; give thanks for all he is going to do for them.

2 Pray in this way for kings and all others who are in authority over us, or are in places of high responsibility, so that we can live in peace and quietness, spending our time in godly living and thinking much about the Lord.

When we pray for those who are in authority over us—our president and even our local officials—we're going to reap tremendous benefits. For example, the decisions made by the leaders of this country affect our economy. And what does the economy affect? It affects you. It affects me. And it certainly affects our paychecks. We need to pray fervently for the people whose decisions have such a powerful impact on our lives!

That puts a different light on our praying, doesn't it? Our officials are sometimes voting on issues that we aren't even aware of. Bills are passed in Congress that we never hear about until after they're already settled. So what do we need to do? We need to pray *continually* for our leaders. Even if we're not aware of the specific issues they are dealing with, we can always pray for the Holy Spirit to direct and guide them—to give them wisdom in every decision they make.

Looking to the Future

Just as it is important that we pray continually for our president and our nation's other leaders, we should also be praying for the future leaders of America. We want to ensure that the right men and women will take office. That means we can't wait until three weeks before Election Day to begin praying. We must start praying now!

Once the Lord prompted me more than two years in advance to begin praying for a particular election. He said to me, "Encourage people to start praying now, because prayer can change the course of things and cause things to be as they should." So everywhere I went during those two years, I urged people to pray for the election.

Of course, we all have our own ideas about who should and should not be in office. However, the words we must always pray are, "God, You know what is best for our country. May Your will be done on earth as it is in Heaven." It's our responsibility to focus on God's Word and pray!

Our Future Is in Our Prayers

My heart is stirred for us as Christians to take our rights, use our authority, and see some wonderful changes in our land. As it says in the Book of Isaiah, God is calling us to be watchmen on the walls of our nation.

ISAIAH 62:6–7 (Amplified)

6 I have set watchmen upon your walls, O Jerusalem, who will never hold their peace day or night; you who [are His servants and by your prayers] put the Lord in remembrance [of His promises], keep not silence,

7 And give Him no rest until He establishes Jerusalem and makes her a praise in the earth.

It doesn't matter how peaceful or full of turmoil things may seem, we always need to pray. We *are* the watchmen on the walls of our nation! We must put the Lord in remembrance of His promises and give Him no rest until He establishes the United States of America and makes her a praise to the earth.

We want America to be a God-fearing land. We want America to be a praise to this earth. America's future—our future—is in our prayers. Let's take this country back to the foundation upon which it was established and believe for a great spiritual awakening to spread across our land!

Prayer Points

I encourage you to use the following prayer points to help you pray for our nation.

- President

- Congress
- Supreme Court
- State and Local Authorities
- Military
- Intelligence Agencies
- Safety of Our Country
- Future Leadership

Remember, as we each take our place and do our part, our prayers will be effective. Our prayers will change laws and circumstances. Our prayers will keep us safe. Our prayers will heal our wonderful land!

CHAPTER 13

Pray Out Your Piece of the Puzzle

Several years ago the Lord gave me a clear visual image of His plan for each and every one of us in the Body of Christ. He said to me, "The work that I have for the Body of Christ to do is like putting together a beautiful puzzle."

Have you ever put together a puzzle? There are so many pieces to a puzzle, but you have to put it together piece by piece. And it takes every one of those pieces to make the puzzle form a beautiful picture.

If you've ever struggled to find one or two missing pieces, you know it can be extremely frustrating. You're so disappointed every time you look at the puzzle. Even though everything else looks pretty, all you can see are the glaring holes where a few pieces are missing.

Sometimes I can picture the Lord as He looks at our puzzle in the Body of Christ. Even though most of the puzzle has been put together and many of us have gotten into place, I can see our Heavenly Father looking at those glaring holes in the puzzle where someone has not taken the proper position.

After the Lord gave me this visual image, He said to me, "In order for what I have for the Body of Christ to be accomplished on this earth, every person has a piece of the puzzle. It's important that each of you takes your piece of the puzzle and accomplishes My will for your life. As that happens on this earth, I am putting together a beautiful picture of My plan."

When you think about the Body of Christ as a puzzle, you can probably picture the grass, sky, trees, and water that make up that puzzle. But we're not just making a beautiful picture to look at. We're making a picture for our God! And we desperately need the people of God to pray out the grass, trees, and sky—the whole picture.

It's your responsibility to pray out your piece of the puzzle, and it's my responsibility to pray out mine. And if we don't pray out our individual parts, there's going to be something missing. We're going to be one of those glaring holes in God's puzzle!

When the Lord gave me this vivid picture of what we as the Body of Christ need to accomplish on the earth, it fit perfectly with what the Apostle Paul said in First Corinthians 12:27—*"All of you together are the one body of Christ and each one of you is a separate and necessary part of it"* (TLB).

Each one of us is a separate and necessary part of the Body of Christ—a separate piece of God's puzzle. You have a part to play and so do I. And we need to understand how important each part is.

Of course, we're living in an age and generation when people want to let everybody else do the work while they sit back and enjoy the results. But God wants all of us to do our part.

ROMANS 12:4–5 (TLB)

4–5 Just as there are many parts to our bodies, so it is with Christ's body. We are all parts of it, and it takes every one of us to make it complete, for we each have different work to do. So we belong to each other, and each needs all the others.

Paul says in these verses that there are many parts in our physical bodies. There's the head. There are the arms, the shoulders, and the legs. And there are also many parts in the Body of Christ. But there shouldn't be any competition in the Body. We each have a gift that God has given us. We each have an important part to play.

Someone might think, "I'm only the little toe." But a toe is very important. Just stump your toe or break it and see how important it is!

One time my husband broke his little toe. I had rearranged the furniture in our bedroom and moved a chair that had been at the foot of our bed. Before we went to bed that night, I had warned Ken, "Honey, that chair is in a different place."

Of course, he reassured me that he would remember. But when he got up in the middle of the night to get a drink of water, all of a sudden I heard, "Owwwwwwwwwwwww!" He had stumped his little toe on that chair and had actually broken it.

That toe may have been small, and it may have seemed as if it wasn't doing a lot of work. But Ken soon found out how important his little toe was when it hurt so badly!

When something happens to your little toe, you feel it. It hurts. And it's the same way in the Body of Christ. Each one of us is important and we each have an assignment from the Lord. You may think, *My assignment is not very important.* But it doesn't matter if you're the arm, the leg, the foot, or the little toe—you're still important. And if the little toe is hurting, we need to minister to the little toe. We all need to minister to one another!

It's Time to Step Into Place

In verses 6 and 7 of Romans chapter 12, the Apostle Paul continues to describe how God has created all the parts of the Body of Christ to function together.

ROMANS 12:6–7 (TLB)

6 God has given each of us the ability to do certain things well. So if God has given you the ability to prophesy, then prophesy whenever you can—as often as your faith is strong enough to receive a message from God.

7 If your gift is that of serving others, serve them well. . . .

So many times we think the gift of hospitality is not as important as the gift of prophecy. But the gift of serving others is one of the most important gifts we could ever have!

ROMANS 12:7–8 (TLB)

7 . . . If you are a teacher, do a good job of teaching.

8 If you are a preacher, see to it that your sermons are strong and helpful. If God has given you money, be generous in helping others with it. . . .

God has blessed some people with a gift that causes everything they touch to prosper. But in many cases, instead of being content to operate in that gift, they desire to preach the

Gospel. They desperately want to be in a pulpit ministry, when their real gift is supporting the Gospel with their finances. But God needs businessmen and businesswomen to support the work of His Kingdom!

ROMANS 12:8 (TLB)

8 . . . If God has given you administrative ability and put you in charge of the work of others, take the responsibility seriously. Those who offer comfort to the sorrowing should do so with Christian cheer.

Notice the second part of verse 8. Have you ever been feeling down and someone made you feel so much better? It wasn't really the words they said or the advice they gave you; it was just the way they comforted you—the hug or the pat on the shoulder. It was their reassurance that you could make it. That's a special gift from the Lord!

God has placed each one of us in the Body of Christ for a reason, and it's time for us to step into the place where God wants us to be. Romans 12:12 tells us, *"Be glad for all God is planning for you. Be patient in trouble, and prayerful always"* (TLB). The *Amplified Bible* says, *"Be constant in prayer."* The *New International Version* tells us, "Be faithful in prayer."

How are we going to accomplish what God has for each one of us in His divine plan? By being faithful in prayer—by praying out our piece of the puzzle. It takes fervent, heartfelt prayer if we want to accomplish the plan of God for our lives!

Connecting With the Heart of God

First Corinthians 2:9 says, " *'No eye has seen, no ear has heard, no mind has conceived what God has prepared for those who love him'* " (NIV). I really want that verse to get hold of you as it has gotten hold of me. You see, the Lord has great things prepared for each and every one of us. And the next verse says, *"But God has revealed it to us by his Spirit."*

Our spirits must commune with God's Spirit if we want to know the great things He has planned for us. How do we commune with the Spirit of God? Through prayer—through talking to Him. As I mentioned in a previous chapter, John 4:24 tells us, *"God is a Spirit: and they that worship him must worship him in spirit and in truth."*

If we want to find out God's plan for our lives, we must connect with the heart of God through our spirits. We must keep our spirits sensitive to the Lord. And we must not grieve the Holy Spirit. It's so important that we stay sensitive to the things of God and obey His voice.

Jeremiah 29:11–13 says that God has good plans for us. But if we want to know those plans, we must seek Him with all of our hearts.

JEREMIAH 29:11–13 (NIV)

11 "For I know the plans I have for you," declares the Lord, "plans to prosper you and not to harm you, plans to give you hope and a future.

12 Then you will call upon me and come and pray to me, and I will listen to you.

13 You will seek me and find me when you seek me with all your heart."

Notice what the Lord says in verse 12—*"Then you will call upon me and come and pray to me, and I will listen to you."* As we listen to the Lord, He listens to us.

Once again God is saying in these verses, "I have a plan for you." And that plan is extremely important to the Lord. But the only way you're going to find out the plan that He has for you is to talk to Him. That's why verse 13 says, "*You will seek me and find me when you seek me with all your heart.*" Praise God, He will listen to us and hear the cry of our hearts as we learn to listen to Him!

Fresh Instructions From the Lord

One of the most important reasons that we must pray is so we can receive God's instructions and follow His perfect will for our lives. He wants to give each and every one of us instructions, even in the daily affairs of life. And as we each pray out our part of the puzzle, my, my, my! What a time we're going to have in the Lord!

We need to receive fresh instructions from God every day. He may have an assignment for us to do on a certain day, but if we're not sensitive to His voice, we won't hear that assignment. It's so important that we train ourselves to be sensitive to the Holy Spirit and instantly obey Him.

As we become willing vessels and allow the Lord to mold us and make us into what He has created us to be, He will lead us, guide us, direct us, and take us down avenues that we had never thought possible. He will open doors of opportunity that we thought were closed forever. But this will only happen as we talk to the Lord and obey His voice.

As you obey the Lord, He will thrust you out into greater circles, into greater realms of opportunity. You will go from one avenue to another, as door after door opens wide for you!

Your Heavenly Father will lead you down a path that you've never thought of before—a path that's well planted, well watered—a path that's flourishing with His abundance. And when the day comes when you stand before the Throne of God in the Heaven of heavenlies, the Father will say to you, "*Well done, thou good and faithful servant: . . . enter thou into the joy of thy lord*" (Matt. 25:21)!

CHAPTER 14

Stir It Up to Win Souls!

"Ask of me, and I shall give thee the heathen for thine inheritance."

—Psalm 2:8

The harvest of souls upon this earth is ripe. But Jesus said in Matthew chapter 9 that the laborers are few. Then He admonished His disciples to pray. What were they supposed to pray? They were to pray for laborers to be sent out into the harvest fields of the earth.

MATTHEW 9:37–38

37 Then saith he unto his disciples, The harvest truly is plenteous, but the labourers are few;

38 Pray ye therefore the Lord of the harvest, that he will send forth labourers into his harvest.

Why are there so few laborers in the Lord's harvest? I'm sorry to say that sometimes the laborers are so busy basking in the blessings God has given us that we don't have time to go out into the world and be witnesses for Him.

Jesus said in Acts 1:8, *"Ye shall be witnesses unto me."* The *New Living Translation* says, *"You will be my witnesses, telling people about me everywhere."*

Do you realize how many people today are lost and going to hell? Do you realize the exciting opportunity we have to tell the world about Jesus? Our first and foremost responsibility as Christians is to go out and proclaim this wonderful Good News—the Gospel!

Where are we going to be witnesses? Wherever God takes us. Each one of us, every day, comes in contact with someone who doesn't know Christ. How sensitive are we to listen to the voice of God and pray for an opportunity to minister to those people? Are we too busy to lend a helping hand to those who are lost, those who are hurting, and bring them in?

You don't know what lies ahead for the person who may be sitting next to you on your job. You don't know if you'll ever see that person again after today. Let me ask you a thought-provoking question. Do you know, if that person were to die today, whether you would see that one in Heaven?

Oh, we have such a revelation of the truth and knowledge of the Word of God, and yet in so many cases, we're keeping it to ourselves. We're not proclaiming it to the world. God didn't give us this knowledge to keep to ourselves but to take to others and be His witnesses. He wants us to go into the highways and byways and compel them to come in!

I know that some people are simply great soul winners. They're extremely bold and they don't mind going up to anybody and asking, "Do you know Jesus Christ as your Savior?"

You may not be comfortable doing that. I know I'm not bold in that way either. But even if we do not have that particular kind of boldness, we can still be witnesses for the Lord. He has called each one of us to be a witness for Him!

I have always been the type of person who endeavors to witness to people by my actions, my love, and my compassion for others. I love people. I love to help people and listen to them. I have a compassion for those in need, and I especially love the ones who are hardened against the Gospel.

Many years ago when we were building the RHEMA campus, I came in contact with a particular supplier who furnished all of our carpet. One of the owners of that company had been saved, and I believe it was in a Pentecostal denomination. But he was not walking in fellowship with the Lord at the time.

In fact, he was a very hard person—deeply hardened against the church. Some things had been done that offended him, so he would always make fun of ministers.

It grieved my heart when I heard him say those negative things, but I didn't try to correct him. I didn't even try to defend anyone. I simply continued to show him the love of God and the compassion that I had in my heart to help people.

At this particular time, I had to stop by this man's business quite frequently, and I usually went around 10 o'clock in the morning. (That's about as early as I like to conduct business in the first place!) But one morning I had so much to do that I stopped by his business around 8 o'clock.

He was absolutely shocked when he saw me that morning, because he knew that was not my favorite time of day. So he exclaimed, "It's 8 o'clock in the morning and you're still smiling and happy!"

Then his business partner remarked, "We have never seen you when you were down. We know that you're not a morning person, but you're still smiling at 8 o'clock in the morning. You must know something that we don't."

What an opportunity he gave me! I mean, he had just asked me a question that I could walk right into and share the Gospel. So I replied, "Most definitely I do know something. Let me tell you what it is." And I began to witness to them about the Lord.

I didn't ask them to pray the sinner's prayer that day, but not long after that the man who had been so hardened against the Gospel came out to the RHEMA campus to see the carpet we had purchased from him. As he toured the campus, we wound up in my husband's office. There on the coffee table was a faith Bible—a Bible with our faith notes printed in it.

As soon as he spotted that Bible, he exclaimed, "I'd sure like to have one of those Bibles!" So we got him a Bible and signed it, and he took it with him.

Several weeks later, I had another contact with this man. You know, when you're fishing for souls, it's similar to fishing for fish. You have to draw in the line a little at a time.

This particular time, I called him on the phone regarding a business situation, and all of a sudden the conversation turned to the Lord. I could feel an urgency inside to draw in the net just a little bit more, so I called him by name and said, "You know, Heaven won't be Heaven if you're not there."

"Lynette," he replied, "I've been reading the Bible you gave me more than you might think." Just at that moment, I wanted to draw in the net all the way, but for some reason, I didn't. I wish I had, because only a week later we received a phone call that this man had suddenly died from a heart attack.

That incident hit me so hard, because I thought, "God, why didn't I make sure that he was right with You?" Of course, I believe that he had accepted Christ as his Savior and that he is in Heaven right now. But I made a point at that very moment to tell the Lord, "I'm not going to let that kind of opportunity pass me by again!"

Day after day, opportunities to witness come to each of us. I encourage you to pray and ask the Lord to open doors for you to present the Gospel in your own way, with your own personality, and in whatever way He desires to use you. When you tell the Lord you want to go fishing for souls, He will make it possible!

A Hungry Fish

A few years ago one of our employees shared a testimony of how he and a friend were at a movie theater, waiting for the movie to start. The people sitting behind them were using such foul language that it was really getting on his nerves. So he turned around and said to them, "I work for RHEMA." Then he began to strike up a conversation.

They immediately told him, "We don't like religion."

Of course, our employee was quick to let them know, "We don't like religion at our church either. We like the move of God. We like the gifts of the Spirit. We cast out devils and pray for the sick." As I listened to him share this part of the testimony, I thought, *Oh my goodness, that kind of talk is going to scare them away!*

But these people suddenly asked him, "Where is your church? We want to go there." So they actually came to church, gave their hearts to the Lord, and later brought some of their friends who also gave their hearts to Christ. Through that one incident, the Lord brought several more souls into the Kingdom of God!

When our employee shared this testimony, I thought, *Wow! That's wonderful, but there's no way unless the Holy Ghost really gets hold of me that I could ever witness in that way.*

All of a sudden my heart was gripped with a desire to have more opportunities to witness to people. You see, in the world I navigate in, most of the people are already Christians. That means I don't have much of an opportunity to come in contact with people who don't know Christ as their Savior. But after I heard that testimony, a prayer started bubbling up in my heart—"God, please send me to people I can witness to, souls I can fish for, someone I can bring into the Kingdom of God."

Only a week or so after I started praying that prayer, God gave me the opportunity I was praying for. My son and I were going to lunch, and I had an important meeting shortly afterward. In fact, I only had 15 minutes for lunch that day.

Craig and I went to a fast-food restaurant just a few blocks away from our ministry offices, and I told him, "I'll jump out and order while you park the car. By the time you get inside, we'll have our food."

So I went in and placed our order. I was so focused on getting our food that I didn't pay much attention to the people behind the counter. I paid for our lunch, got the cups for the drinks, and went over to the soda fountain to fill them.

All of a sudden, I heard this voice calling my name. It sounded like someone whom I hadn't seen in years—perhaps an old, close friend. I'm thinking, *This must be a roommate I had in college years ago.*

So I looked around to see where this voice was coming from, and it was one of the ladies behind the counter. I acknowledged her and smiled, and then she said, "I know who you are. I watch you on television."

I'm thinking, *Oh, no! Please don't bother me right now. I only have 15 minutes to get back to the office. This is not the time for you to give me your testimony or ask me a question about the Bible.* But, thank God, I didn't say what I was thinking. Sometimes it's best for the thoughts that come into our heads not to come out of our mouths!

Now I usually love talking to people, and I don't mind people talking to me. I'm normally very patient and I gladly listen to whatever someone wants to tell me. But that particular day was not one for small talk! In fact, I wanted to get as far away as I possibly could from this voice that was calling my name. So I thanked the woman for watching me on television and hurried to sit down.

Craig and I took our food over to the farthest corner of the restaurant and began to conduct our business while we ate lunch. All at once I noticed this lady wiping the table next to us, even though it was already clean. It was obvious that this was really a hungry fish!

Finally she said to me, "You must be very busy."

"Well, yes, I am," I replied with a smile. "I do have quite a lot to do." So she walked away again, and I thought, *Praise the Lord. I'm going to get out of here without offending anybody and I'll get to my meeting on time.*

My son and I had just finished eating when all of a sudden this woman started getting a little bolder. She said to me, "I have a problem. Can you help me?"

As soon as those words came out of her mouth—*boom*—I remembered my request to the Lord. I knew this was my moment that I had been praying for. This was my opportunity to witness for Him.

Suddenly it didn't matter if I had a meeting scheduled in two minutes. It didn't matter what happened the rest of the day. All that mattered to me was that I had prayed and asked God to give me an opportunity to be a witness, and here it was!

So I quickly began to ask the Lord, "God, I need You to give me wisdom and tell me what to say. Please help me because this is a fish that I don't want to lose!"

Have you ever gone fishing in the natural, and you felt a tug on your line and you knew it was a big fish? You jerked the line to set the hook, but you didn't jerk it hard enough. And suddenly that big fish flopped off your line! It upset you, didn't it? Sometimes that's the way it is when we're reeling in souls for the Lord Jesus Christ.

So I asked the Lord, "What should I say to catch this fish?" You see, for different types of fish you have to use different methods of fishing. You don't fish for crappie the same way you fish for catfish, do you? You don't use the same bait for both types of fish if you want to catch anything.

Similarly, we can't use the same method in witnessing to everyone we come in contact with. Some methods will turn people away. That's why we always need to be sensitive to the Spirit of God.

So I asked this woman, "What is your problem?"

"Well, I once knew Christ," she continued, "but I'm an alcoholic, and I've had trouble with this all of my life. Every time I try to walk with the Lord, I wind up getting back on the bottle. Not only that, but I smoke, and I can't seem to stop. I just want to have victory in my life! Can you help me?"

"Most definitely I can," I told her.

Then I asked her if she had gone to church recently, and she gave me all kinds of excuses. So I urged her to get back into church. Next I told her, "We have a class at our church that I believe can help you. It's called Turning Point, and it meets every Sunday before the church service. It's a class to help you turn your life back over to Christ. They will help you in your walk with the Lord so you won't fall back into these temptations."

As I began to describe to her where our church was, something on the inside was telling me, "She'll never come if you just tell her where the church is. You'll have to oversee this person. You need to have someone meet her at the church."

So I said to her, "Tell me your name and phone number," and she quickly told me that her name was Nancy. "I'm going to have someone call you," I replied. "They will make arrangements to meet you and show you where the class is." I knew in my heart that if I didn't do this, I was going to lose this fish.

I called the teacher of the Turning Point class and told her, "I have another fish for you!" Then someone from the class made the connection with her. She came to church the next Sunday morning, and she went down to the altar and rededicated her life to Christ. I saw her in our church services later, praising and worshipping the Lord.

When I asked Nancy's teachers about her, they said, "Oh, she's a joy to the class. She really inspires the others."

I kept checking on her, and if I didn't see her at church I would call her and say, "Nancy, where are you? I haven't seen you lately."

Every time I did see her at church, she would tell me, "Oh, I just love this church. Everybody is so friendly and helpful."

Each time Nancy came out the door after the services, she would always hug my neck, and I noticed that her clothes were completely saturated with cigarette smoke. It was several months later when I suddenly realized that I didn't smell smoke on her clothes anymore.

Praise God, all of those fetters that had bound her for so long were being broken! Why? Because she was hearing the Word of God and there were people surrounding her, helping her, praying for her, and discipling her. If we'll lead them to the Lord, He will clean them up!

Occasionally Nancy would call our office and ask to talk to me. Even when I was in the midst of a busy week, I realized that she was my responsibility—she was "my fish"—and I would talk to her.

One time she called on a day when I was stuck in one meeting after the other. So my assistant invited Nancy to come and talk with her. Nancy told her, "When I called your office, the choice was either call you or hit the bottle." How important it is for us to respond to the cry of someone who is reaching out to the Lord!

We never know when God is going to ask us to go fishing for Him. When I think about the day I met Nancy, I realize how badly I could have messed up my fishing trip for the Lord because of my busy schedule. It's so important for us to have a desire to go fishing for souls and to pray and ask the Lord to give us the opportunities!

Pray for the Rain of the Spirit

What is God waiting for in this hour? He's waiting for souls—for the precious fruit of the earth. Do you remember the verse we read in James chapter 5? It says, *"Be patient therefore, brethren, unto the coming of the Lord. Behold, the husbandman waiteth for the precious fruit of the earth, and hath long patience for it, until he receive the early and latter rain"* (v. 7).

We're living in a season of the harvest of souls. But before we can have a harvest, we have to have rain. So I encourage you, first of all, to pray for the rain of the Holy Spirit to bring in a mighty harvest. Deuteronomy 11:14 says, *"I will give you the rain of your land in his due season, the first rain and the latter rain, that thou mayest gather in thy corn, and thy wine, and thine oil."* In other words, God is saying, "I will give you rain so you may gather in the harvest."

Next, it's important for us to pray for healings and miracles. We should not be satisfied until we see the power of God in full demonstration in this hour. We should not be satisfied until we see the things we read about in the Bible happen today. The Word says that Jesus Christ is the same, yesterday, today, and forever (Heb. 13:8). If He healed yesterday, He'll heal today. If miracles were performed yesterday, we can expect miracles to be performed today.

My heart longs to see the lame walk, the deaf hear, and the blind see. I so desire to see people in wheelchairs walk out of those wheelchairs. And I'm desperate to see the things that occurred in the Early Church happen today. We need to pray for signs, wonders, and miracles to confirm God's Word. Those are the things that will draw people to the Gospel!

Pray for the Lost

It's also important for us to pray for the lost. I remember how my Aunt Oma prayed for many years for her father's salvation. He had deserted their family right after my father was born. But in his later years, he came to live with Aunt Oma and her sister.

My grandfather had never been close to the Lord. He had never lived a godly life. He had once known the Lord, but if you tried to talk to him about God, he would just argue the Bible with you. It was awful!

Near the end of his life, Aunt Oma prayed for him day in and day out. She told the Lord, "I'm not going to let him die until I know I'm going to meet him again in Heaven one day."

Several years passed as she reminded God of His Word and prayed fervently for my grandfather. But he was still chewing tobacco and arguing the Bible. All of a sudden, at the age of 96, he stopped chewing tobacco, which was a habit he had enjoyed for many years. That was a miracle in itself, but something else changed. Instead of arguing about the Bible, he wanted to talk about the things of God. He desired to know more about the Word. Aunt Oma knew that he had had a change of heart.

He was such a proud man that he would never admit, "I'm right with the Lord." But all the signs were there that he had made things right with his Maker. When Aunt Oma was finally certain that he was saved, she told the Lord, "Father, You can take him home now because I know I'm going to meet him again one day."

Within one week's time, my grandfather went home to be with the Lord. Thank goodness, God honors our prayers when we pray for the lost to be saved!

Are You Ready to Draw in the Net?

As I mentioned at the beginning of this chapter, we also need to pray for laborers to go out into the harvest. And that means we must be willing to be the one who is sent!

Are you ready to be a laborer—a witness for the Lord? We are here on this earth to carry the Gospel of the Lord Jesus Christ all over the world.

I encourage you today to make a rededication in your heart that you will get back to the Great Commission, to that to which you were first called. I want that desire for souls to well up inside you so much that you'll wake up every morning and pray, "Lord, where can I be a witness for You today?"

I believe the fire of God is going to burn so strongly in your heart that you will go out and be a witness for Him in all of your world. I encourage you to pray, "God, give me a greater passion for souls." And when you pray that prayer, He will grant the desire of your heart.

That's what is going to bring the King back—when we, the people of God, stir ourselves up to win souls and the whole world hears that Jesus Christ is Lord. I believe we've already stepped into the edge of that last, great-day revival, but we must not stop. We must press in. We must stir ourselves up to pray—because this last great move of God is being birthed by prayer.

I'll tell you, in these dark days and perilous times, I've never been so excited in all of my life. Why am I excited? Because we're going to go out and be fishers of men. And we're not going to be able to catch them all with just one line. We're going to have to draw them in with a net!

Are you ready to do that? It only comes when the people of God pray. You see, it's prayer that fuels the fire. It's prayer that ignites revival. And it's continuing in prayer that will cause this revival to explode!

Are you willing to join me and be one of God's channels to pray for this last, great-day revival? Are you ready to enlist to pray for a mighty harvest of souls? I want to pray for you right now:

"I thank You, Father, that the fire of Pentecost is being reignited in us today. The message of faith is being reignited in our hearts. May there be a rejuvenation, a fresh enthusiasm, and a passion for souls in the hearts of Your people. I thank You that the passion we once had will return to us.

"Lord, give us a hunger for Your Word and a desire to draw closer to You. May we have a strong desire to know You more, to seek Your face, and to stir up that holy fire in our souls, because we have a mighty work to do—and it all begins with prayer. Amen."

Friend, there may be strongholds that have held you for so long. Perhaps they've kept you from getting closer to the heart of God. They keep pulling you back every time you try to move forward. I take authority over those things, in the Name of Jesus, and I believe the Lord is saying to you today, "Those strongholds are broken!" Just boldly proclaim, "I am free!"

There shall be a freedom in your life that you have not experienced before.

You will walk in a light that you have not walked in before.

You will see things in a different light, and the glory of God will be manifested in your life.

The fire that's burning in your heart will soon begin to spread.

It's going to spread to your neighbors.

It's going to spread to your city.

It's going to spread to your state.

It's going to spread to your country.

It's going to spread to every country on this earth!

When that same kind of fire is stirred up in believers all over the world, the Lord Jesus Christ will come back and we will have that great Marriage Supper of the Lamb. Oh, what a celebration that will be! As we each take our place as God's messengers and proclaim the Gospel to every creature, the Father's mighty plan will be accomplished on this earth!

Salvation Prayer

Perhaps you've never talked to God or given your heart to Him. Or you may have once walked with the Lord but you need to rededicate your life to Him.

Our Heavenly Father loves you so much and He wants to have a close relationship with you. You can call upon Him today and know that He will answer you. It's that simple! All you have to do is pray this prayer from your heart:

Dear God,

I come to You in the Name of Jesus.

Your Word says, "*The one who comes to Me I will by no means cast out*" (John 6:37 NKJV). According to Your Word, You won't cast me out, and so I thank You for taking me in.

You said in Your Word, "'*Whoever calls on the name of the Lord shall be saved*'" (Rom. 10:13 NKJV). I am calling on Your Name, and I believe You are saving me.

You also said, "*If you confess with your mouth the Lord Jesus and believe in your heart that God has raised Him from the dead, you will be saved. For with the heart one believes unto righteousness, and with the mouth confession is made unto salvation*" (Rom. 10:9–10 NKJV). God, I believe in my heart that Jesus Christ is Your Son. I believe that You raised Him from the dead, and I confess Him now as my Lord and Savior. According to Your Word, I am now saved! Thank You, Heavenly Father!

Notes

[1] C. Austin Miles, 1912, "In the Garden." Public Domain.

[2] "God's Voice Mail," http://www.sermonillustrator.org/illustrator/sermon1/god's.htm.

[3] J. Oswald Sanders, *Spiritual Leadership*, rev. ed. (Chicago: Moody, 1980), 121.

[4] Cleavant Derricks, "Just a Little Talk with Jesus." Copyright © 1937 Bridge Building Music (BMI). All rights reserved. Used by permission.

[5] Dwight L. Moody, *Prevailing Prayer: What Hinders It?* (New York: Fleming H. Revell Co., 1885).

[6] "Christian Prayer Quotes," http://www.christian-prayer-quotes.christian-attorney.net/.

[7] E. M. bounds, *E. M. Bounds on Prayer* (New Kensington, PA: Whitaker House, 1997), 11–12.

[8] http://thinkexist.com/quotation/by_perseverance_the_snail_reached_the_ark/147376.html.

[9] Frederick C. Mish, ed., Merriam-Webster's Collegiate Dictionary, 11th ed.(Springfield, MA: Merriam-Webster, Inc., 2004), 491.

[10] Strong's Greek Dictionary, #4856 *sumphōneō.*

[11] "The Great Awakening of 1857–1858." http://smithworks.org/revival/1857.html.

[12] "Facts and Firsts," Joint Congressional committee on Inaugural Ceremonies, http://inaugural.senate.gov/history/factsandfirsts/index.cfm.

[13] "Franklin's Appeal for Prayer at the Constitutional Convention," Wallbuilders, http://www.wallbuilders.com/LIBissuesArticles.asp?id=98.

"What should I do with my life?"

If you've been asking yourself this question, **RHEMA BIBLE TRAINING COLLEGE is a good place to come and find out.** RBTC will build a solid biblical foundation in you that will carry you through—wherever life takes you.

The Benefits:

- Training at *the* **top Spirit-filled Bible school**
- Teaching based on steadfast faith in God's Word
- Unique two-year core program specially designed to **grow** you as a believer, help you **recognize the voice of God**, and equip you to **live successfully**
- Optional **specialized training** in the third- and fourth-year program of your choice: Biblical Studies, Helps Ministry, Itinerant Ministry, Pastoral Ministry, Student Ministries, Worship, World Missions, and General Extended Studies
- **Accredited** with Transworld Accrediting Commission International
- Worldwide **ministry opportunities**—while you're in school

WORKING *together* TO REACH THE WORLD!

People. Power. Purpose.

Have you ever dropped a stone into water? Small waves rise up at the point of impact and travel in all directions. It's called a ripple effect. That's the kind of impact Christians are meant to have in this world—the kind of impact that the Rhema family is producing in the earth today.

The Rhema Word Partner Club links Christians with a shared interest in reaching people with the Gospel and the message of faith in God.

Together we are reaching across generations, cultures, and nations to spread the Good News of Jesus Christ to every corner of the earth.

To join us in reaching the world,
visit **rhema.org/wpc** or call **1-866-312-0972**.

Always on.

For the latest news and information on products, media, podcasts, study resources, and special offers, visit us online 24 hours a day.

rhema.org

Free Subscription!

Call now to receive a free subscription to *The Word of Faith* magazine from Kenneth Hagin Ministries. Receive encouragement and spiritual refreshment from . . .

- *Faith-building articles from Kenneth W. Hagin, Lynette Hagin, Craig W. Hagin, Denise Hagin Burns, and others*
- *"Timeless Teaching" from the archives of Kenneth E. Hagin*
- *Feature articles on prayer and healing*
- *Testimonies of salvation, healing, and deliverance*
- *Children's activity page*
- *Updates on Rhema Bible Training College, Rhema Bible Church, and other outreaches of Kenneth Hagin Ministries*

Subscribe today for your free *Word of Faith*!

1-888-28-FAITH (1-888-283-2484)

rhema.org/wof

OFFER CODE—BKORD:WF

Rhema

Correspondence Bible School

The Rhema Correspondence Bible School is a home Bible study course that can help you in your everyday life!

This course of study has been designed with you in mind, providing practical teaching on prayer, faith, healing, Spirit-led living, and much more to help you live a victorious Christian life!

Flexible

Enroll any time: choose your topic of study;
study at your own pace!

Affordable

Profitable

"The Lord has blessed me through a Rhema Correspondence Bible School graduate. . . . He witnessed to me 15 years ago, and the Lord delivered me from drugs and alcohol. I was living on the streets and then in somebody's tool shed. Now I lead a victorious and blessed life! I now am a graduate of Rhema Correspondence Bible School too! I own a beautiful home. I have a beautiful wife and two children who also love the Lord. The Lord allows me to preach whenever my pastor is out of town. I am on the board of directors at my church and at the Christian school. Thank you, and God bless you and your ministry!"

—D.J., Lusby, Maryland

"Thank you for continually offering Rhema Correspondence Bible School. The eyes of my understanding have been enlightened greatly through the Word of God through having been enrolled in RCBS. My life has forever been changed."

—M.R., Princeton, N.C.

For enrollment information and a course listing, call today!

1-888-28-FAITH (1-888-283-2484)

rhema.org/rcbs

OFFER CODE—BKORD:BRCSC